WINE
East of the Rockies

BY HUDSON CATTELL and LEE MILLER

Presenting Pennsylvania Wines

The Wines of the East:
  The Hybrids
  The Vinifera
  Native American Grapes

Wine East of the Rockies

WINE
East of the Rockies

by Hudson Cattell and Lee Miller

L & H Photojournalism · 1982
Lancaster, Pennsylvania

Production coordinator: Linda Jones McKee
Design, layout and map: Marian Broderick
Production assistants: Susan Cottrel and John P. Herr
Printing by Stauffer Printing Service, Inc., Lancaster, Pa.:
  J. Richard Stauffer, president; Jan McComsey,
  production manager; Janet McComsey, typesetter
Binding by Optic Graphics, Inc., Glen Burnie, Md.
Jacket photo by Wayne Broderick
Jacket printing by Acorn Press, Lancaster, Pa.:
  Donald K. Roseman, president

Library of Congress Cataloging in Publication Number:
82-90971
ISBN 0-911301-00-3

Copyright © 1982 by L & H Photojournalism
All rights reserved
Manufactured in the United States of America

L & H PHOTOJOURNALISM
620 North Pine Street
Lancaster, Pennsylvania 17603

Preface

Many years ago, while working on a newspaper story, we sat down with Tom Hampton in his southern Lancaster County farmhouse. Tom opened a bottle of his excellent homemade Chancellor and began pouring out his enthusiasm for winemaking and grape growing. This was not only our introduction to wine, but our first contact with something new called the Eastern wine industry. Tom and his wife Cindy went on to establish their own winery, Tucquan Vineyard, and we went on to follow and record much of the progress of this new industry.

It is now our turn to share, and we hope that some of the excitement we felt on that first day is evident in these pages. The East is still young enough that the reader who wishes to take the time to explore one of the world's newest wine regions can experience the same excitement we did. On the other hand, Eastern wines have reached the point where many of the crisp, light whites can hold their own with similar wines from anywhere in the world, and where the best of the reds show the promise of one day being eagerly sought by wine lovers everywhere.

Today there are nearly 350 wineries in the East, and the number is increasing with every month that goes by. It has been impossible to do more in this book than to try to capture the nature of the Eastern wine experience today. Each winery has its own individual and interesting story to tell and, regrettably, not every winery or person involved in the industry could be included. We made the decision to present an overview of the East rather than a detailed study, and our sincere apologies go to many friends who could not be included here. For the reader, this may be a plus: part of the excitement of the Eastern wine experience can only be obtained by visiting a winery one knows absolutely nothing about prior to entering its driveway.

In a way, we are a bit envious of our readers. The experience that awaits you is one we have had, but can never repeat.

Hudson Cattell

July 24, 1982

Lee Miller

Acknowledgments

All of the photographs in the book were taken by Hudson Cattell with the exception of those otherwise credited here.
Photos by John P. Herr include: Lemon Hill on page 15, the winery interior and exterior at Tucquan Vineyard on page 45, the publications on page 123, the magazine cover on page 124, and all photos on page 125. Linda Jones McKee took the following photos: Peaceful Bend Vineyard on page 36, the barrels on page 43, Tom and Cindy Hampton on page 45, Jim Held on page 51, Allegro Vineyards on page 67, Eric Miller on page 68, Cascade Mountain Vineyards and William and Margaret Wetmore on page 71, Byrd Vineyards and Bret and Sharon Byrd on page 77, Antuzzi's Winery and Matthew Antuzzi on page 78, Tewksbury Wine Cellars on page 78, Murli Dharmadhikari on page 86, Alexis Bailly Vineyards and David and Nan Bailly on page 86, St. James Winery and Jim and Pat Hofherr on page 87, Mount Pleasant Vineyards on page 87, the Bucks Country Vineyards extension on page 92, Elmer Swenson on page 108, and the harvest photo on page 129. Michael B. McKee took the pictures of the arches and winery at Stone Hill Wine Company on page 51 and the Golden Rain Tree Winery on page 86.

The photos of Bill Moffett, Hope Merletti and Richard Figiel on page 124 were supplied by *Eastern Grape Grower and Winery News*, the photo of Valley Vineyards on page 84 by Marge Schuchter, and the commemorative plate for Dr. Frank on page 30 by Gary Woodbury. Sam Melhorn took the pictures of the Post Winery and the restaurant of Wiederkehr Wine Cellars on page 88, and Al Cabral the photo of Rico's Winery on page 90. The picture of Bobby Smith on page 90 was furnished by La Buena Vida Vineyards, and Diane Rushing supplied the photos of the winery and members of her family on page 82.

We should like to thank Dick Sherer of Hammondsport, New York, for permission to draw upon his collection of Finger Lakes memorabilia for the Great Western poster on page 19, the Pleasant Valley and Highland Cottage labels on page 20, the Funkheimer label on page 21, the Pleasant Valley juice label on page 25, and the photo of the Taylor brothers on page 41. The photo of the Urbana Wine Company exhibit on page 20 is used by courtesy of Charles Fournier as is the picture of the historic Gold Seal bottles on page 31. The early Brights' labels on page 29 are reproduced through the courtesy of Brights Wines, and Jim Held of the modern Stone Hill Winery supplied the photo of the label of the old Stone Hill Winery on page 20. Dr. Angus Adams sent us the ad for Turner's Invalid Tonic on page 25, and Elisabeth Woodburn kindly allowed us to photograph her historical pictures of the Brotherhood Winery on pages 21 and 42.

Frederick Trench Chapman gave us permission to use his illustration of Tyrkir discovering grapes that appears on page 13; the illustration first appeared in *Voyages to Vinland: The First American Saga* by Einar Haugen (New York: Alfred A. Knopf, 1942). The quotation on page 14 by George F. Williston is from *Saints and Strangers* (New York: Reynal and Hitchcock, 1945). Tom O'Grady of Rose Bower Vineyard and Winery gave us

permission to include the poem on page 93, published originally as poem number 33 in a collection, *Establishing a Vineyard/Pour Realiser un Vignoble* (Paris: Editions Saint-Germain-des-Pres, 1978).

A number of the photographs in the book appear without captions. Some need further identification. The photo opposite the title page was taken at Truluck Vineyards at sunset; the barn on page 35 is the home of Pennsylvania's York Springs Winery; the ecstatic winemaker on page 109 is Dick Nissley of Nissley Vineyards in Bainbridge, Pennsylvania, at the exact moment his name was announced as an award winner at Wineries Unlimited; the tasting room on page 114 is at Wagner Vineyards in Lodi, New York; and the young lady modelling the T-shirt on page 151 is Kharran Cattell. Most of the other pictures are timeless and, with variation, appear time and again in the East.

We would like to thank all of the individuals and organizations listed above for their cooperation in making this a better book. Many other people deserve credit for the time they took to answer questions, furnish labels and verify facts: the list of names is virtually endless, and we would like to extend our sincere appreciation to all who helped.

Although we have not seen the finished book as these words are written, it is obvious that many people involved in the production of this book have spared no effort to make the final product as attractive as possible. Two people in particular have gone far beyond the call of duty, and we would specifically like to thank Marian Broderick for her uncompromising approach to design and layout, and Linda Jones McKee for so expertly carrying out her dual task of production coordinator and book editor.

Table of Contents

INTRODUCTION ... 8

A WINE REGION CALLED THE EAST ... 10

THE EARLY DAYS ... 13
- Of Vikings and Pilgrims ... 14
- Days of Glory ... 18
- The Curtain Falls ... 23
- Out of the Darkness ... 26
- Four Men Who Made It Happen ... 27

THE EAST TODAY: WINERIES AND WINE PEOPLE ... 33
- The East Today ... 34
- A Region of Contrasts ... 36
- Among the Largest ... 38
- On a Smaller Scale ... 43
- Some That Came First ... 49
- The Newcomers ... 66
- A Wine Tour of the East ... 69
- From All Walks of Life ... 91

THE EAST TODAY: THE SUPPORTING CAST ... 101
- Introduction ... 102
- Research and Extension Work ... 103
- Conferences and Societies ... 109
- Tastings ... 114
- Fairs and Festivals ... 118
- Publications ... 123

THE WINES OF THE EAST ... 127
- Introduction ... 128
- White Table Wines ... 130
- Red Table Wines ... 137
- Rosés ... 143
- Non-Varietal Wines ... 145
- Varieties with a Past ... 146
- Fortified Wines ... 147
- Sparkling Wines ... 148
- Fruit Wines ... 150

THE CREATIVE TOUCH ... 151

APPENDIX: THE WINERIES OF THE EAST ... 155

*Joseph Lembo, Lembo Vineyards,
Lewistown, Pennsylvania*

Harvest. Bone tired.
For many hours, the pickers have been out in the vineyards fighting off sweat and yellow-jackets, filling baskets that are emptied into one-ton bins. A steady stream of grapes arrives at the winery where the crusher-stemmer devours the fruit and spews it out into fermenting tanks. At midnight grapes are still being processed. No time for rest for man or machine.

Winter. Bitter cold.
With pruning shears, men and women walk through the vineyard rows, breath condensing in the frigid air, trying to keep the numbness out of their bones. The vines stand there, seemingly lifeless, defenseless as the limbs of a year's growth are cut and discarded into mounds of brush that soon dwarf the newly thinned vines. No time or effort is wasted as experienced hands quickly judge the proper number of buds to leave behind for a new season's health and vigor.

Spring. Growth.
Endless hours in the vineyard trying to keep back weeds, masterminding the arduous spray schedule that will second-guess nature and make the difference between a good harvest and a poor one. It is warm, even hot in the vineyard, and there is a feeling of life, of something being born from the soil.

Scenes from around the world, wherever wine is made.
Endlessly, the grapes are planted, harvested and made into wine. It is work, but out of that work will come pride. The feeling of creating a bottle of wine that someone else will pick up and open one night to grace a meal. And joy. The joy of making something with one's own hands, mind, heart.

Challenge and reward. The artist at work.
Whether it be in Michigan or Maryland, Massachusetts or Arkansas, Ontario or South Carolina, challenge and reward have created the wine region of eastern North America. At hundreds of wineries in the East, bottles of wine are filled, corked and capped. Finally, a label is applied. The label is an imprimatur. It tells where the wine has come from, who has made it. It is a signature, and each signature is different from any other signature anywhere else in the world.

While the East is generally described as that part of North America east of the Rocky Mountains, grape growing and winemaking tend to be concentrated in certain parts of this vast region. The shaded areas on the map indicate the areas where wineries have been established.

A Wine Region Called the East

The wine producing areas of the eastern United States and Canada known as "the East" cover a broad expanse of the North American continent from the Rocky Mountains to the Atlantic Ocean, and from the Gulf of Mexico to southern Canada. Within these boundaries are 350 wineries and tens of thousands of acres of grapes.

Just as California has its Napa Valley and Central Valley, and just as France has its Burgundy and Bordeaux, so the East, too, is often broken down into smaller districts. These may be identified by political boundaries such as the Virginia or the Ohio wine industry, or in geographical terms such as the Finger Lakes of New York or the Niagara peninsula of Ontario.

In other cases, common soils and climatic conditions unite wineries across state boundaries as, for example, the Lake Erie region consisting of parts of Pennsylvania, New York, and Ohio. As viticultural designations are approved by the United States government, other descriptive phrases — such as Lancaster Valley in Pennsylvania, or Augusta in Missouri — are coming into existence.

But despite its broad territory and the wide variety of its climates, soils and geographic features, there are common bonds that weld the East into a unique wine region. One of these is the challenge in nearly every area of having to cope with difficult growing conditions. Another common tie is the similar grape varieties grown throughout the East, a number of which are not grown anywhere else in the world.

Also uniting the wineries of the East is the "newness" of the industry itself. Today's intense interest in winemaking and grape growing has largely come about in the last 25 years, and the industry as a whole is in the same general stage of development. Winemakers and growers from all over the East come together for wine competitions and tastings. They compare wines, exchange ideas and share technical information. Through their efforts, individually and collectively, the East is today becoming recognized as one of the world's major wine growing regions.

The Early Days

Of Vikings and Pilgrims

Part of the colorful story of grapes and wine in the East lies in the past. There are those who say it started in the year 1000 when Leif Eriksson and a band of Viking companions first discovered grapes growing wild along the North Atlantic coast.

One evening it happened that one of their crew was missing, a man named Tyrkir the German. Leif . . . prepared to leave with a search party of twelve. But when they had gone only a short way from the house, there was Tyrkir walking towards them. Leif saw at once that he was in high spirits.

"Why are you so late, foster-father?" Leif asked. "How did you get separated from your companions?"

At first Tyrkir talked for a long time in German, rolling his eyes and making faces. No one could understand a word he said. After a while he changed over to Norse.

"I went little further than the rest of you, yet I have some real news for you. I found grape vines and grapes!"

"Is this true, foster-father?" Leif asked.

"Certainly it is true," he replied. "I was born where vines and grapes are no rarity."

They slept that night, and in the morning Leif said to his crew, "We now have two jobs to do. One day we shall gather grapes, and on the other day cut vines and chop timber to provide a cargo for my ship."

This they did, and it is said that their towboat was loaded with grapes and the ship itself with a cargo of timber. In the spring they made the ship ready and sailed away. Leif named the country after the good things they found in it, and called it Vinland (Wine-Land). They put out to sea and had favorable winds until they came in sight of Greenland and its ice-capped mountains.

This narrative, preserved in Iceland as part of *The Greenlander's Saga*, is the first reference to grapes and wine in the history of North America. The Vikings returned home, America was forgotten, and the next mention of grapes and wine does not occur until after the rediscovery of America by Columbus nearly 500 years later.

The first permanent English settlement in North America came in 1607 at Jamestown, Virginia. Captain John Smith, leader of the expedition, kept track of the early progress of the Virginia colony. Both grapes and wine were included in his description written in 1609.

Of vines, great abundance in many parts, that climbe the toppes of the highest trees in some places, but these beare but fewe grapes. But by the rivers and Savage habitations where they are not overshadowed from the sunne, they are covered with fruit, though never pruined nor manured. Of these hedge grapes, wee made neare 20 gallons of wine, which were neare as good as your French British wine. . . .

In 1620 the Mayflower landed in Plymouth, Massachusetts, and the first Thanksgiving was celebrated by the Pilgrims in 1621. According to some accounts, wine was served at that first Thanksgiving day feast. In his 1945 study of the Pilgrims, *Saints and Strangers*, George F. Willison describes that historic occasion:

Captain Standish staged a military review, there were games of skill and chance, and for three days the Pilgrims and their guests gorged themselves on venison, roast duck, roast goose, clams and other shellfish; succulent eels, white bread, corn bread, leeks and watercress and other 'sallet herbes,' with wild plums and dried berries as dessert — all washed down with wine, made of the wild grape, both white and red, which the Pilgrims praised as 'very sweete & strong.'

If, in fact, wine was served at that first Thanksgiving, it is the first record we have of wine complementing food in the New World. It is easy to imagine how a touch of the grape made life in the wilderness a little easier to bear.

The first grape vines from Europe to be brought into the colonies arrived in 1619 under the auspices of Lord Delaware (3), governor of the Colony of Virginia. Another well-known attempt was made by William Penn (2) who planted his vineyards in Philadelphia in 1684 on what is known today as Lemon Hill in Fairmount Park (1).

1, 2. Pierre Legaux's house in Spring Mill, Pennsylvania, is still standing, although the original winery building has long since been replaced by a firehouse.
3. Stock certificates issued by the Pennsylvania Vine Company survive, this one being issued late in the company's history.
4. Thomas Jefferson (1743-1826), the third president of the United States, is well remembered today for his interest in wine.

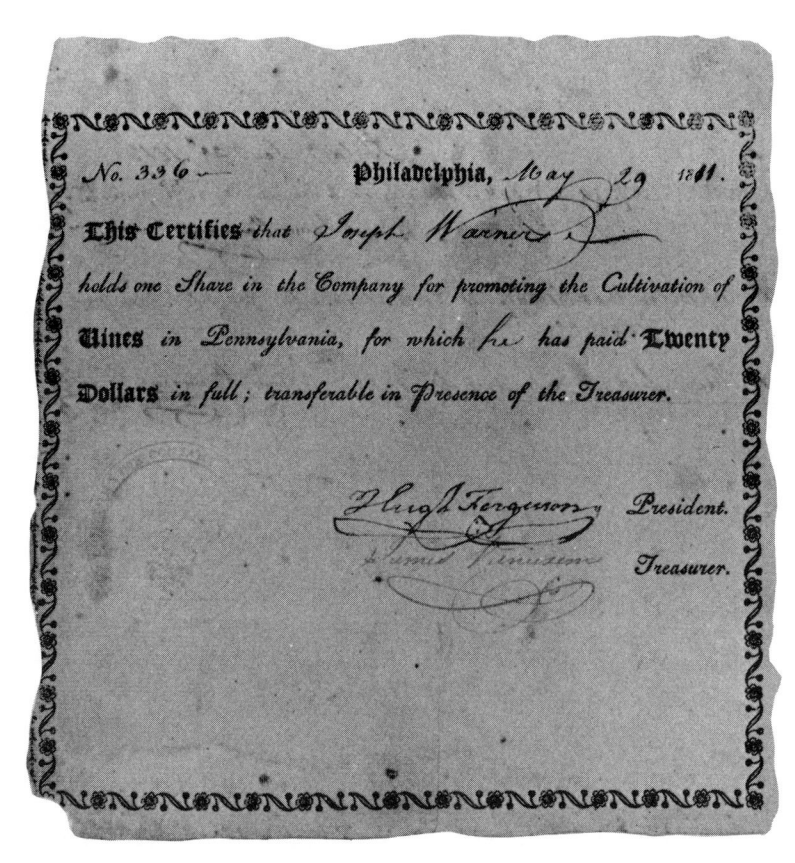

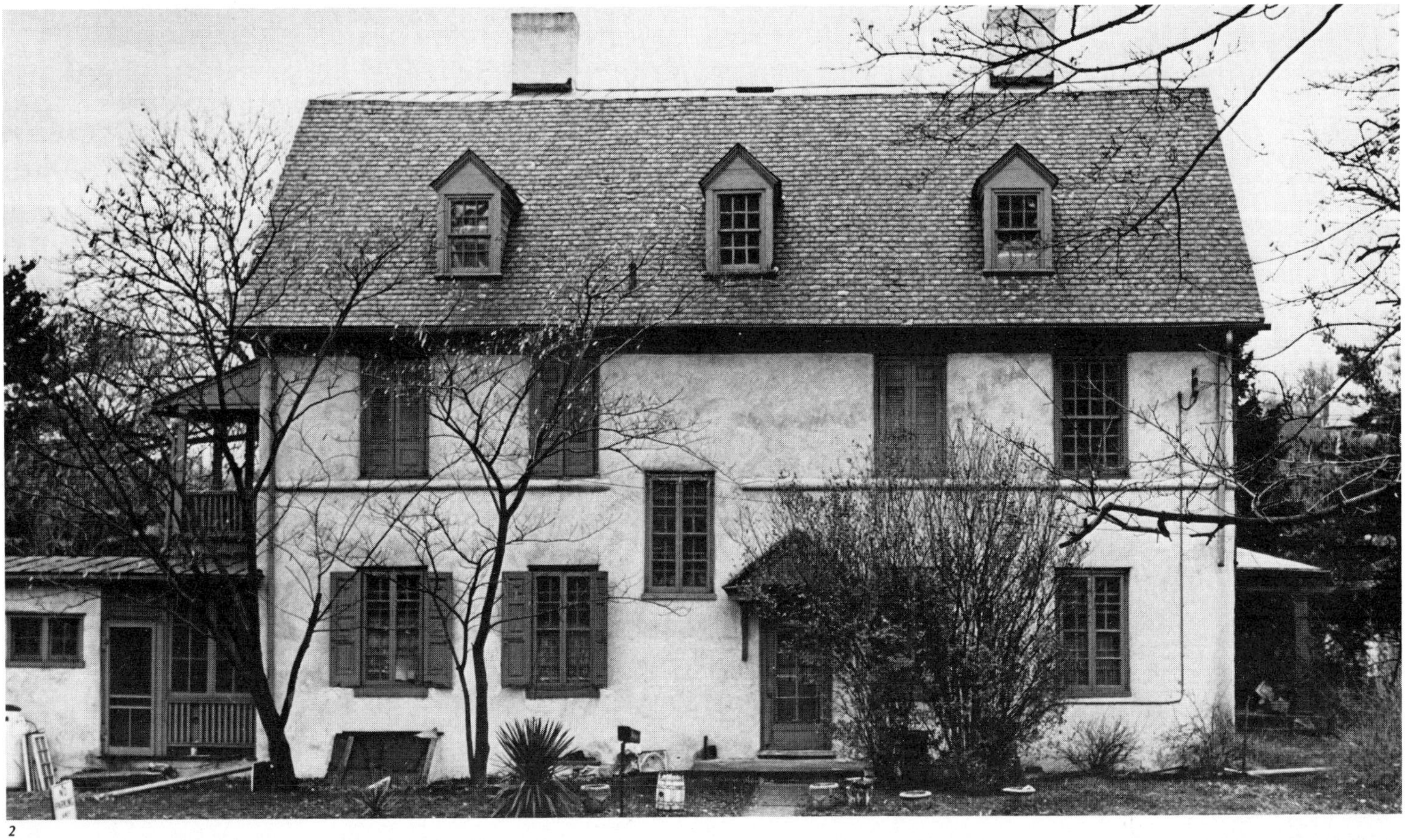

Another early account of wine feasts dates back to 1716 when Virginia Colonial Governor Spotswood and his "Knights of the Golden Horseshoe" headed west to the Shenandoah Valley, accompanied by their attendants. The attendants would be sent on ahead to prepare a campsite and, after a leisurely day's ride, the party would arrive in high spirits ready for an evening of feasting and wine. When the excursion ended and the gentlemen had returned, little golden horseshoes were made up and presented to each of the participants.

Throughout the Colonial period, new settlers brought vinifera grape vines with them from Europe and tried to establish vineyards based on these grapes. A combination of harsh winters, insects and disease prevented many of these early colonial vineyards from surviving even long enough to bear a crop. The home winemaking industry that subsequently grew up in many parts of the East had to be based on the hardy native species of grapes that flourished in the wild. Another source of supply was found by the Moravians of eastern Pennsylvania who made wines from currants and other fruits for use in religious ceremonies.

The first commercial vineyard in the United States was established north of Philadelphia at Spring Mill in 1793. Pierre Legaux, a friend of the Marquis de Lafayette, established a private stock corporation called the Pennsylvania Vine Company to finance the vineyards. While many varieties were planted, the only one to prove successful was the Alexander grape, a cross between a wild vine and one of the vinifera varieties that had earlier been brought from Europe.

Many of the prominent Americans of the day bought stock in the Pennsylvania Vine Company, including Alexander Hamilton and Aaron Burr. Among others attracted to the quality of wine made from the Alexander grape was the third president of the United States, Thomas Jefferson.

Jefferson's interest in wine was of long standing. As ambassador to France he had brought back with him the finest wines he could find. At his home at Monticello he attempted to grow vines brought from Europe for more than 30 years before admitting failure. After tasting wine made from the Alexander, he wrote, "the wine of this was as good as the best Burgundy and resembling it." Familiarity with the Alexander probably helped him reach a conclusion he expressed in 1808: "We can produce in the United States as many varieties of wines as Europe does; not the same ones, but undoubtedly of the same quality."

While the Alexander grape itself was not enough to save the Pennsylvania Vine Company from failure at the time of the War of 1812, it did play a further role in Eastern wine history. Vines from Legaux's vineyard were taken west to Kentucky, Indiana and Ohio. It was in the Cincinnati area that the commercial wine industry of the East first achieved success.

Days of Glory

In 1859, Ohio was the largest wine producing state in the United States. Its production of 570,000 gallons represented more than one-third of the national total and more than twice the amount produced in California, then just getting started with its own industry. By 1871, the Golden Eagle winery on Middle Bass Island in Lake Erie was the largest winery in the nation, making over 500,000 gallons a year.

In these years before 1900, wines from Ohio, Missouri and New York dominated the Eastern wine scene. They competed directly in the best restaurants with wines from Europe, and they achieved international recognition. In 1873, a Great Western champagne from New York State became the first American "champagne" to win a gold medal in Europe when it was placed in competition at the Vienna Exposition. Two Gold Seal champagnes entered by the Urbana Wine Company of New York (now Gold Seal Vineyards) won medals at the Paris Exposition in 1879 at the first head-on competition between American and French sparkling wines. In Paris, Brussels, Philadelphia and Chicago, Eastern wines scored success after success in international competition. As late as 1900 at the Paris Exposition, where American wines won 36 medals and 4 honorable mentions, the awards list included five wines from New York, two from Ohio, and one each from Florida, New Jersey, North Carolina, Virginia and the District of Columbia.

The Lonz winery (2) is located on the site of the Golden Eagle Winery, built by Andrew Wehrle in the 1860s. The original cellars remain, but the present Gothic castle was constructed during the 1930s and 1940s. A magnificent view of Lake Erie (1) can be seen from the tower.

This ad for Great Western champagne (3) appeared in the April 3, 1915 edition of Puck.

1

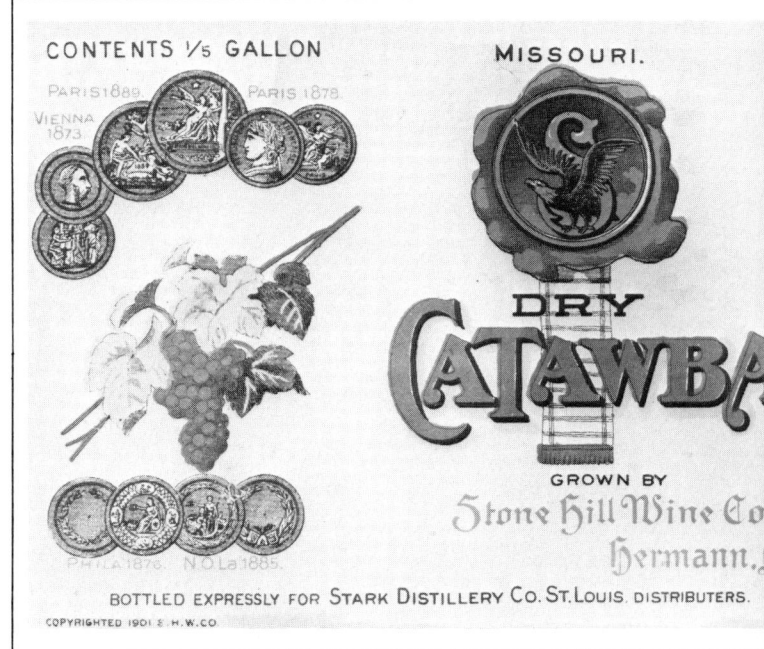
3

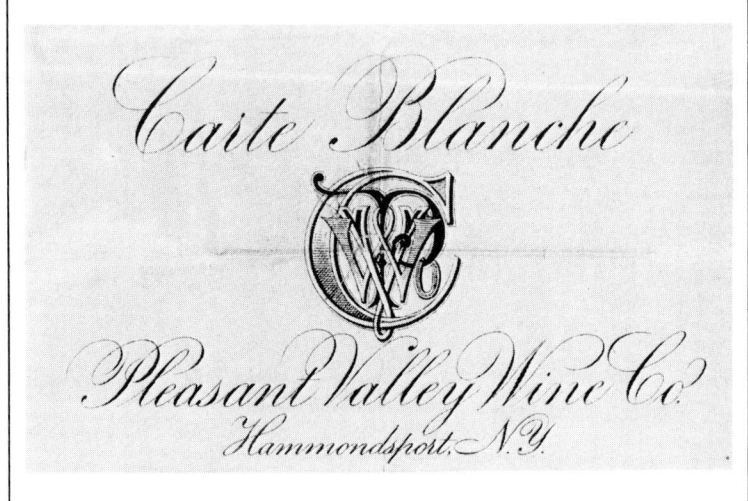
2

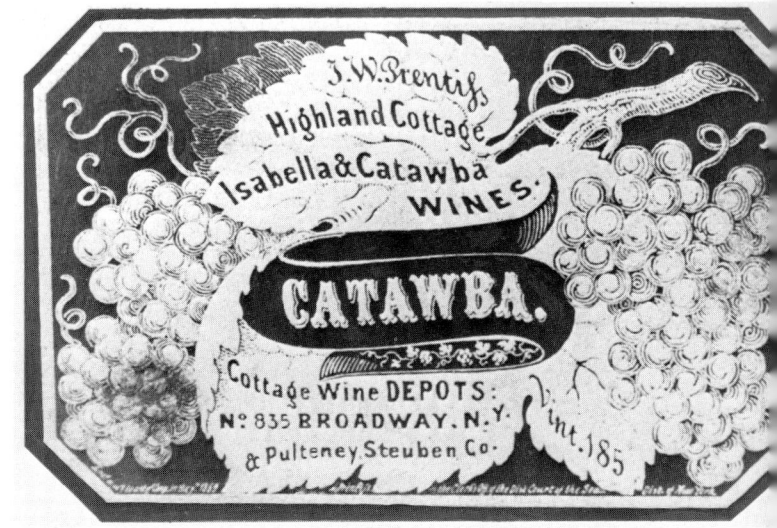
4

A few labels, photographs and brochures have survived from the past of Eastern wines. Although they seem quaint today, they reflect the work and pride that went into winemaking in the decades before Prohibition.

(1) The Urbana Wine Company, now Gold Seal, had a booth at the World's Columbian Exposition held in San Francisco in 1893. This picture of the booth appeared on the front page of Scientific American on September 16, 1893.

(2) The Pleasant Valley Wine Company, now part of The Taylor Wine Company, was founded in 1860, and the label shown here was used in the middle of the last half of the 19th century.

(3) Between 1873 and 1904 Stone Hill Winery in Hermann, Missouri, won eight gold medals at world's fairs. These medals were used as part of the design on their labels.

(4) Little is known about the Highland Cottage winery in the Finger Lakes, but they obviously marketed in New York City. The date on the label was printed 185_ so that it could be used for several years. A faint "8," not visible here, indicates that the label was intended for use in 1858.

(5) The winemaking operations of Brotherhood Wine Company were (and still are) located at Washingtonville in the Hudson River Valley. The cover of this old price list shows that Brotherhood had its own sales office in New York City.

(6) Oldtimers in Hammondsport recall that the wines of Funks' Wine Cellar had a devoted following. The Funkheimer label was probably developed before Prohibition and its use continued afterwards.

All of the wines of this era were made from native American varieties of grapes. The native American varieties were crosses between the wild grape species that had been growing when the first settlers arrived in North America and the vinifera that had been brought from Europe; some of these were "chance" hybrids that had occurred naturally in the wild, and others were man-made crosses at the hands of American hybridizers. An 1880 account lists the most important of these varieties as being Catawba, Isabella, Delaware, Iona, Walter and Concord.

Catawba, the first of these varieties to become commercially significant, was discovered growing in the wild in North Carolina about 1802. By mid-century the variety had achieved prominence, largely through the efforts of one man, Nicholas Longworth (1).

Longworth moved from New Jersey to Cincinnati, Ohio, in 1804 and quickly made his fortune in real estate. He planted his first vineyards in 1813, but his real success began in 1825 when he received cuttings of Catawba. By 1850 his plantings had expanded to more than 40 acres, and his Catawba wines were being marketed throughout the United States. In Europe, Longworth won critical acclaim for his Sparkling Catawba, the first champagne to be produced in the United States. By 1859 more than 2,000 acres of Catawba were

1

planted in the Cincinnati area, and Longworth's winery had been joined by a dozen others.

Catawba and other native American varieties were responsible for what might be called a "golden age" for Eastern wines. That age began to draw to a close in the late 1800s, however, when many vineyards succumbed to diseases for which sprays had not yet been invented.

Competition also played its part. The wine industry in California entered a boom period in the 1880s and 90s, and by the end of the century, California was the leading wine producing state. The biggest blow came in 1920 with the advent of Prohibition.

The Curtain Falls

"After one year from the ratification of this article, the manufacture, sale or transportation of intoxicating liquors within, the importation thereof into, or the exportation thereof from the United States and all territory subject to the jurisdiction thereof for beverage purposes is hereby prohibited."

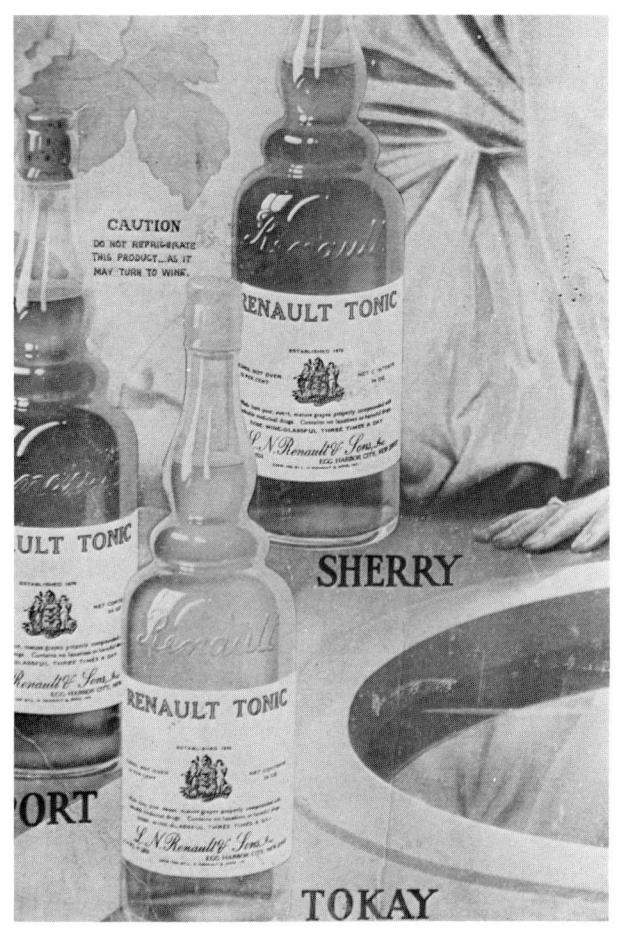

1

The terse words of the 18th Amendment to the Constitution of the United States became the law of the land one year after ratification on January 29, 1919. Winery after winery closed its doors, and state after state was left without an operating winery. Only a few of the larger wineries survived by converting to grape juice processing or to the production of the legal kinds of wine that could still be made, such as communion wine for use in religious services and medicinal tonics.

The coming of Prohibition lowered a curtain on Act I of the Eastern wine industry. At the time, few would have guessed that there would be an Act II, let alone that the Eastern wine industry would rise from the ashes as fast as it did.

2

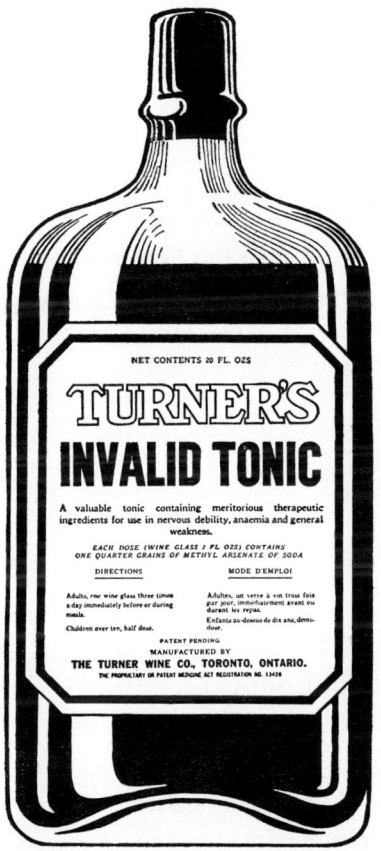

ESTABLISHED 1860 / ETABLIE 1860

TURNER'S INVALID TONIC

TURNER'S Invalid Tonic is a valuable tonic preparation. It is especially indicated in conditions such as anaemia, debility, general lassitude, loss of appetite, weakness and fainting spells, nerve exhaustion, torpid liver, and convalescence from influenza, pneumonia or other debilitating and exhausting diseases. As a basis it contains rich red wine which for generations has been recommended by physicians and largely used by people in all walks of life as a restorative and stimulating tonic. To this wine has been added other valuable medicinal ingredients each of which has for many years been employed on account of its special tonic properties. Thus the combination results in a reliable general tonic of much merit. For the most satisfactory results Turner's Invalid Tonic should be used according to the directions on the label and the use of it continued until the body has regained its normal tone.

LE tonique Turner pour Invalides est une préparation tonifiante de grande valeur. Il est spécialement recommandé dans les cas d'anémie, débilité, lassitude générale, perte d'appétit, faiblesse et chocs nerveux, épuisement nerveux, foie inactif, convalescence, à la suite d'influenza, pneumonie ou autres maladies qui causent la débilité et l'épuisement. Il est à base de riche vin rouge que les médecins recommandent depuis des générations et que boivent les personnes de toutes professions comme tonique pour restaurer et stimuler. A ce vin ont été ajoutés d'autres excellents ingrédients médicinaux utilisés depuis des années pour leurs propriétés toniques spéciales. Le produit qui en résulte donne un tonique général de grand mérite. Pour obtenir les meilleurs résultats du Tonique Turner pour Invalides, il faut le prendre d'après les directions sur l'étiquette et continuer d'en prendre jusqu'à ce que la santé soit redevenue normale.

The Turner Wine Company
104-106 Front St. E., TORONTO, Can.

3

4

Some wineries, such as the Pleasant Valley Wine Company, survived Prohibition by marketing grape juice (4). Others, including the Renault Winery in Egg Harbor City, New Jersey (1, 2), turned to medicinal tonics which were sold in drug stores. Recommended dosage was a "wine-glassful three times a day," and a cautionary note appeared prominently: "Do not refrigerate this product... as it may turn to wine." Refrigeration did indeed cause the medicinal elements to settle to the bottom of the bottle, leaving a 22% alcohol wine.

Prohibition in Canada lasted from 1916 to 1927 and, as in the United States, both beer and liquor were banned. However, wines produced in Canada were exempted, and Canadian wine became the only legal alcoholic beverage in the country. Under the provisions of the Ontario Temperance Act, wine could only be sold at the winery in minimum quantities of five gallons or two case lots. Turner's Invalid Tonic (3), designed to be sold in drug stores, was one of the ways in which it remained possible to sell small quantities of wine in retail outlets.

Out of the Darkness

When Prohibition came to an end in the United States in 1933, there was no immediate resurgence of interest in grape growing and winemaking. The few wineries in existence were larger ones that managed to stay in business making sacramental wines or medicinal tonics. Among these were The Brotherhood Wine Company in Washingtonville, N.Y., founded in 1839 as Blooming Grove; the Pleasant Valley Wine Company of Hammondsport, N.Y., established in 1860; The Taylor Wine Company of Hammondsport, founded in 1880; Gold Seal Vineyards of Hammondsport, started in 1865 as the Urbana Wine Company; Widmer's Wine Cellars of Naples, N.Y., dating back to 1888; and Renault Wine Company of Egg Harbor City, N.J., founded in 1868.

The end of Prohibition in Canada, ironically, led to the closing of many of the Canadian wineries that had flourished during Prohibition. Strict standards on wine quality and winery sanitation were adopted in the mid-1930s that only a few wineries could meet. The number of wineries in Ontario dropped from 51 to less than ten, and the first new winery licenses were not approved until the mid-1970s.

The emergence of today's small, premium wineries in the United States did not begin until after World War II, and, for the most part, not until the late 1960s and the decade of the 70s. As might be expected, the opening of these wineries occurred after the planting of new vineyards in the East. These new plantings contained grape varieties not available in the earlier golden age of Eastern viticulture. The development of modern sprays and fungicides now made possible the growing of the vinifera varieties that had failed so miserably in colonial times. Available also were new hybrids developed in France in the late 1800s which combined some of the delicate flavor characteristics of the vinifera with the hardiness of the native American varieties. Both the vinifera and French hybrid grapes could be used to make dry table wines, whereas the native American varieties were primarily suited for making sweeter wines, sherries and champagnes.

Winemaking in some states began earlier than in others where laws had to be changed. In many states pressure had to be brought on legislatures to pass laws permitting the existence of today's small wineries.

One of these early boutique wineries was High Tor Vineyards, founded by Everett Crosby in 1952 along the Hudson River 35 miles north of New York City. In a book, *The Vintage Years,* he describes the hardships, the bureaucratic obstacles and the rewards of being a pioneer. For advice and recommendations on which grapes to plant, Everett Crosby turned to Philip Wagner, one of several men who were to shape the directions of the modern Eastern wine industry.

Four Men Who Made It Happen

Charles Fournier (1), George W. B. Hostetter (4), Philip Wagner (3), Konstantin Frank (2). Through their dedication, expertise and strength of personality, these men were a primary influence on those who participated in the rebirth of the Eastern wine industry. They not only provided guidance, but gave a whole generation of new Eastern grape growers and winemakers the inspiration to persevere. Not surprisingly, all four were closely involved with the vinifera and French hybrid grapes that were to become the cornerstone of the modern Eastern wine industry.

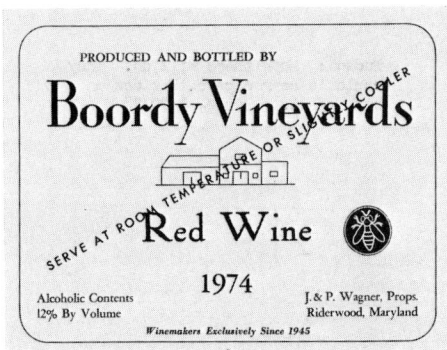

Philip Wagner was a career journalist for the Sunpapers in Baltimore and eventually retired as editor of both the *Sun* and the *Evening Sun*. When he was sent to London in 1936 as a foreign correspondent, he already had a well-developed interest in wine. His first book on American wines and winemaking, published in 1933, was then the only book on the subject available in English. During his stay abroad he became aware of the French hybrids being grown in Europe, and saw the viticultural and winemaking potential for these grapes in the East.

Upon Philip Wagner's return from Europe in 1937 he began planting a vineyard with all of the French hybrid varieties he could find. This led to the establishment of a nursery operation and, in 1945, a winery known as Boordy Vineyards. From the start, Boordy was a partnership between Philip Wagner and his wife, Jocelyn (1). The Baco Noir produced by Boordy in 1945 was the first commercial varietal wine to be produced from a French hybrid grape variety in the East. For many years afterwards, the Wagners' home in Riderwood, Maryland, was a "must" stop for anyone interested in growing grapes in the East or making wines from the French hybrids. Among the many awards received by Philip Wagner was the 1981 Distinguished Award of the Eastern Section of the American Society of Enologists, presented by then-president, Dr. Robert Beelman (2).

1

2

George W. B. Hostetter started learning about viticulture in the 1930s under the tutelage of his father who was chief viticulturist for Brights Wines, established in 1874 in Niagara Falls, Ontario. He had a theory that through the proper use and application of the modern sprays and fungicides then available, it would be possible to grow vinifera grapes successfully in the East.

His chance to prove the theory came in 1946 when Brights ordered a large shipment of vinifera vines from France and established the East's first commercial vinifera vineyard. This planting led to the first commercial vinifera wine produced in the East, a 1955 Pinot Champagne (2). Bright's also produced the East's first vinifera varietal, a Pinot Chardonnay, in 1956 (3). George Hostetter donned an American Wine Society T-shirt while judging the amateur wine competition at the Society's 1981 annual meeting (1).

3

29

Dr. Konstantin Frank was born and educated in Russia and began his viticultural career in the Ukraine. As a wartime refugee from both Russia and Nazi Germany, he escaped to Austria and eventually landed penniless in the United States. His belief that only vinifera grapes could be used in producing the highest quality wine amounted to a passion, and when he had the chance in 1953 to join Gold Seal Vineyards in Hammondsport, New York, to work with Charles Fournier on a program of growing vinifera, he quickly accepted.

The next few years proved that the vinifera could be grown in New York, and in 1957 Dr. Frank planted his own vineyard and established Vinifera Wine Cellars, his own winery. From the start, Dr. Frank was an outspoken champion of the vinifera and advocated growing them with every resource at his command. He welcomed all who came to him for advice and expertise on growing vinifera. In the 1960s, the porch of his Hammondsport house (1) became the birthplace of the American Wine Society.

In honor of his 80th birthday on July 4, 1979, a group of his "co-operators" presented Dr. Frank with a commemorative silver plate (3). Another honor came when The Vinifera Wine Growers Association in Virginia recognized his contributions by naming Dr. Frank the first recipient of their Monteith Trophy. With Dr. Frank in this picture (2) are R. de Treville Lawrence, Sr., president of the Vinifera Wine Growers, and Elisabeth Furness, owner of Piedmont Vineyards and Winery.

Charles M. Fournier was the chief winemaker at Veuve Clicquot Ponsardin in France when, in 1934, he came to the United States to become production manager at Gold Seal Vineyards and to rebuild Gold Seal after the years of Prohibition. When he retired as active president of the winery in 1967 to assume the title of honorary lifetime president, he had done just that. In 1936, he experi-

mented with the French hybrids; in 1943, he introduced his own blend of champagne; in 1953, he hired Dr. Frank to build a vinifera program at Gold Seal; and in 1960 he marketed the first commercial vinifera wines in New York, a 1960 Pinot Noir and a 1960 Pinot Chardonnay (2).

A testimonial to the quality of wine coming from the new Eastern wine industry came in 1950 when the competition at the California State Fair in Sacramento was opened to out-of-state wines. The Charles Fournier New York State Champagne won the only gold medal awarded, and in no year since then has the competition been opened to non-California wines. Charles Fournier is shown here (1) accepting an award at Wineries Unlimited.

The East Today: Wineries and Wine People

The East Today

A few Eastern wineries date back to the last century, a few more to the early post-World War II days, and another handful opened their doors in the 1960s. Starting in the 1970s, the trickle turned into a flood. A typical pattern that emerged was a single individual or family who first planted grapes on their property in the early years of the 1970s, and then opened a winery in the mid-70s. By late 1982, there were nearly 350 wineries between the Rockies and the Atlantic Ocean.

With the numbers came the changes and growth necessary to propel the infant industry into a new stage of richness and sophistication: technological advances and more interest in research, the development of new wine types, the support of local communities and more help on a political level, as well as attention from the media.

Gradually the rugged individualists and modern day "pioneers" were joined by men and women from all backgrounds and walks of life that included doctors, artists, lawyers, architects, business people, poets, writers, farmers, engineers and scientists. They planted vineyards and opened wineries for all kinds of reasons. For some it was simply a hobby, for others an interesting retirement career; some saw it as an investment opportunity as American wine consumption continued to increase dramatically; others, seeking a change in lifestyle, were lured by the romance or the challenge of man against nature; a few had grown up with wine in their blood.

With their diversity came a new kind of professionalism. Through university research and extension work and private consultants, potential vineyard sites were located, and the wine varieties identified that would grow best there. Many winery owners took enology courses and from time to time brought in experienced winemakers from other wine producing areas. Product lines were expanded and marketing became a major consideration as new wineries side-stepped years of gradual increases in production by starting on a larger scale with 20,000 or 30,000 gallons of wine or more. Vineyards were established as businesses, not simply as a source of supply for a winery, while elsewhere wineries opened with no vineyards of their own.

The variety of the wine experience in the East today is as diverse as a group of totally independent-minded people can make it. The scope of the modern-day Eastern wine industry can be seen in the pages that follow.

1

2

4

3

A Region of Contrasts

1. Oasis Vineyards, Hume, Virginia
2. Doerflinger Wine Cellars, Bloomsburg, Pennsylvania
3. Four Chimneys Farm Winery, Himrod, New York
4. Peaceful Bend Vineyard, Steelville, Missouri
5. Wagner Vineyards, Lodi, New York
6. Mt. Hope Estate and Winery, Cornwall, Pennsylvania
7. T. G. Bright and Co., Niagara Falls, Ontario

Among the Largest

The largest wineries in the East make millions of gallons of wine a year and rank with the largest in the world. Everything about these wineries is big, from the size of their tanks to their physical plants and tasting rooms. Some are large corporations in their own right, while others are subsidiaries of major companies. For the most part, these larger wineries are located in the long-established grape growing areas of the East such as the Finger Lakes of New York, the Niagara peninsula of Ontario, western Michigan and southern Ohio. Like large wineries everywhere, they have broad product lines and market over a wide geographical area.

5

Huge quantities of grapes pour into the East's largest wineries at harvest time. At Widmer's Wine Cellars (2) in Naples, New York, one of many arriving bins is dumped into the crusher. The mammoth outdoor tanks at Canandaigua Wine Co. (1), Canandaigua, New York, dwarf the tractor-trailer load of grapes. Canandaigua is the fourth largest winery in the United States, producing over 18 million gallons of wine a year.

The sheer volume of wine produced at the largest Eastern wineries necessitates vast production and storage facilities. Jordan & Ste. Michelle Cellars (5), owned by Carling O'Keefe Ltd., is located in St. Catharines, Ontario, and has storage capacity of 8,000,000 gallons; St. Julian Wine Co. (6) in Paw Paw, Michigan, was founded in 1921 and has storage capacity of 1,500,000 gallons; Chateau-Gai Wines (3) of Niagara Falls, Ontario, founded in 1890, is owned by John Labatt, Ltd., and has storage capacity of 4,500,000 gallons; Gold Seal Vineyards (4), in Hammondsport, New York, is owned by Seagram Co., Ltd., and has storage capacity of 3,000,000 gallons.

6

The number of visitors handled each year at the big wineries is reflected in the size of their tasting rooms. Warner Vineyards (3) in Paw Paw, Michigan, has a separate building used as a tasting room and an adjoining railway car where motion pictures are shown. The large tasting room at T.G. Bright & Co. (2) in Niagara Falls, Ontario, features paneling made from large Douglas Fir tanks once used in the winery. Canandaigua Wine Company's tasting room (1) is located just outside the entrance to Sonnenberg Gardens, a popular tourist attraction across town from the winery's production facilities.

Wine history was made in New York in 1977 when The Taylor Wine Company (1, 2, 3) of Hammondsport was purchased by the Coca-Cola Company of Atlanta. The winery, founded by Walter Taylor in 1880, had previously made headlines in the business press in 1961 when the founder's sons, Fred, Greyton and Clarence (4), decided to sell stock in the winery to the general public. In so doing, Taylor became the first major winery in the United States to go public. Coca-Cola's acquisition followed the death of the last of the brothers in 1976.

The oldest active wineries in the United States and Canada can be included in the list of larger wineries in the East. Barnes Wines in St. Catharines, Ontario (4), founded in 1873, is the oldest winery in Canada still in operation. Standing beneath the massive roof beams at Barnes is chemist Nick Opdam (3). In the United States, the distinction of being the oldest active winery belongs to the Brotherhood Corporation in Washingtonville, New York, dating back to 1839 (1). Originally known as Blooming Grove, the winery was renamed Brotherhood upon its sale in 1885. The appearance of the grounds today (2) contrasts with the quiet scene shown in the turn-of-the-century photograph of the entrance to the main wine cellars.

On a Smaller Scale

In contrast to the "giants" of the industry are the tiny Eastern wineries whose annual production can be measured in the hundreds of gallons, or a few thousand at most. While some of these wineries intend to remain small, others will expand as time goes by.

One characteristic the small Eastern wineries have in common is that they are one-man or family operations where the proprietors generally grow their own grapes and do everything from winemaking to bottling to manning the tasting room. Most of the small owner/operators concentrate on the kinds of wines they personally want to make or those that are in demand in their local markets. Size, however, is not necessarily a limiting factor, as many of the wines from these small wineries have won important medals in wine competitions.

Mawby Vineyards

With sales of approximately 400 gallons a year, L. Mawby Vineyards in Suttons Bay, Michigan, lays claim to being the smallest winery in the East. Proprietor Larry Mawby (1) helps out with the family fruit farm in addition to growing grapes, making wine, and marketing his output. Larry has not yet charted a definite course for the future. Any expansion of the winery will be deferred until he decides which grapes will grow best in his area and which grapes will produce the wines he wants to make. The winery is located in the house Larry designed and built himself (2).

Tucquan Vineyard

Tom and Cindy Hampton (2) have grown wine grapes longer than anyone else in south central Pennsylvania. Ten years after planting grapes in 1968, they opened a winery, Tucquan Vineyard (1), near Holtwood, Pennsylvania. Their intent was to remain small, but they have seen their production gradually increase from 2,000 to 4,000 gallons as the demand for their wines continues to outstrip their ability to produce it. Like many other small winery owners, Tom and Cindy both hold outside jobs and fit in the winery and vineyard work whenever their busy schedules permit. Cindy mans the tasting room (3) occupying the main floor at Tucquan.

Prudence Island Vineyards

Bill Bacon (2), his wife Natalie, and two sons moved to Prudence Island in the middle of Narragansett Bay, Rhode Island, after Bill gave up a career in industry. Life at Sunset Hill Farm (1) is unhurried, but the days are long and busy. There are 16 acres of grapes to tend and a nursery operation to maintain in addition to the winemaking. The main winery building (3), now nearing completion, took four years to build because a shale hillside had to be blasted away to make room for it. "I" beams and eight tons of 3/4 inch reinforcing rods had to be brought to the site by barge. There is no bridge to the island, and public transportation is limited to the Prudence Island Ferry. All wines leaving the winery are carried by the ferry enroute to their Rhode Island destinations.

Stonecrop Vineyards

Tom and Charlotte Young operate Stonecrop Vineyards in Stonington, Connecticut. They planted eight acres of grapes (4) in 1977 and opened their winery two years later. Wine is made in a former two-car garage (2) to the side of their old farmhouse (3), built in 1750. The tasting room is located on the first floor of the house, and a stairway (1), here occupied by son Matthew, leads to a second floor loft which houses works by local photographers.

Biltmore Estate

A small winery can seem large, especially when the small winery has as its sales room the 250-room French chateau-like mansion (1) built in Asheville, North Carolina, by the grandson of Commodore Cornelius Vanderbilt. An experimental planting of grapes was made in 1972 by William A. V. Cecil, a great-great-grandson of the Commodore. By the end of the decade, there were 15 producing acres of grapes and a small winemaking operation. A decision was then made to expand, and the first 120 of a projected 250 acres of grapes (2) were planted in the years 1980 to 1982. The experimental winery, now producing the 2,000 gallons of wine sold at the estate, will be permanently housed in a complex of buildings once used for the farm offices (3). By 1984, this small winery will be in full production — and will no longer be small.

Some That Came First

Throughout the East there are certain people who may be classified as the "elder statesmen" of the Eastern wine industry because of the influence they have had on others. Their long experience in grape growing and winemaking often dates back to an early contact with Philip Wagner or Konstantin Frank in the late 1950s or 1960s, and the practical knowledge they have accumulated over the years has been a major resource for those who followed in their footsteps. They were among the first to plant grapes or make wine in their particular areas and they have often been responsible for taking the lead in securing legislation to permit the establishment of farm wineries or limited wineries in their states. Having come "first," the boutique wineries they established are among the better known wineries in the East.

The Wollersheim Winery

Count Agoston Haraszthy, known today as the father of the California wine industry, started his first winery in the territory of Wisconsin near the town of Sauk City in 1842. The hillside cave probably dug by him for use as an aging cellar (1) may be seen by visitors touring the modern-day Wollersheim Winery. The winery building (2) was built in the years 1859-67 by Peter Kehl for use as a winery and remained in operation until 1899. Bob and JoAnn Wollersheim (3) bought the property in 1972 from the Kehl family and founded the Wollersheim Winery a year later.

Stone Hill Wine Company

Stone Hill Winery in Hermann, Missouri, was started in 1847 and for a time after the Civil War was the second largest winery in the United States, producing more than 1,000,000 gallons. Between 1873 and 1904 their wines won eight gold medals at various world fairs and expositions. In 1965, the first of Missouri's premium wineries opened under the same name on the site of the original Stone Hill Winery. The old office building (1) is currently used as the winery. A series of arched walls going up the hillside (2) show where the old winery building once stood, and the extensive underground cellars are again being used for wine storage. Today's proprietors, Jim Held (3) and his wife Betty, have created a thoroughly modern winery that is now the largest of Missouri's "domestic" wineries.

Bully Hill Vineyards

In terms of mass publicity, few wineries in the East have received the attention from the media that has been accorded Bully Hill Vineyards in Hammondsport, New York. Chiefly responsible for this is Bully Hill's proprietor, Walter S. Taylor (3), one of the most colorful personalities in the world of wine. As an artist, writer, winemaker, outspoken critic and showman, Walter has kept himself and Bully Hill constantly in the public eye.

Walter, whose grandfather was the founder of The Taylor Wine Company, opened his own winery in 1970 after being fired from the family winery for publicly attacking some of its practices. Causes have always been close to Walter's heart. Located on the hillside near the winery — high above Lake Keuka and far from the nearest train track — is this railway tank car (4) which Walter had placed there as a way of protesting the use of out-of-state blending wines in New York.

The Bully Hill complex includes the Greyton H. Taylor Museum (1), named for Walter's father. In addition to the museum on the second floor, the first floor houses Walter's artwork. Omission of the name Taylor on the main building (2) is part of a long standing controversy and legal battle between Walter and The Taylor Wine Company over an acceptable use of the Taylor name. During the time when use of the Taylor name was being litigated in the courts, Walter Taylor designed a number of distinctive labels (5) for use by Bully Hill Vineyards.

Benmarl Wine Company

No sharper contrast to the flamboyance of Bully Hill could be found than in the dignified atmosphere of Benmarl Wine Company in Marlboro, New York, operated by Mark and Dene Miller. Mark Miller was a top magazine illustrator in the 1950s when he fell in love with wine while living and working in the wine regions of France. He first envisioned growing grapes on their property overlooking the Hudson River in the mid-1950s, and, together with Dene and their two sons, Eric and Kim, opened what was to become New York State's first farm winery in 1971.

Borrowing an old Burgundian tradition, the Millers established the Société des Vignerons, a privately subscribed society in which members purchase "vine-rights" entitling them to the production of two grape vines from the estate vineyards. Each member's wines are privately labeled (1).

Mark Miller (4) originally designed the sculpture of the Benmarl angel as a doorpull for the winery, and it has since become a symbol of the Société. Behind him are various illustrations of his that appeared in leading magazines of the 1950s. The Benmarl buildings surrounding a central courtyard were designed by Dene Miller (2, 3).

4

Montbray Wine Cellars

One of the first people to be directly influenced by Dr. Konstantin Frank was Dr. G. Hamilton Mowbray (3), an experimental psychologist in the applied physics laboratory at Johns Hopkins University in Baltimore. Following his initial visit to Hammondsport in 1958, he planted his first vineyards in Silver Run Valley, Maryland, a year later. Montbray Wine Cellars ("Ham" uses the original French version of the family name) opened in 1966 (2). A sharp freeze early in October, 1974, enabled him to make the first commercial Ice Wine ever made in the United States (1).

Presque Isle Wine Cellars

Douglas P. and Marlene Moorhead (3) are the proprietors of Presque Isle Wine Cellars in North East, Pennsylvania. Coming from a grape growing family (his father brokered grapes in New York and Ohio), Doug became interested in winemaking early in the 1960s while serving in the United States Army in Germany. Presque Isle Wine Cellars (1, 2), originally a partnership with William Konnerth, opened in 1964 to sell home winemaking supplies and juice. Together with other Erie County grape growers, Doug and Marlene helped lead the fight to secure passage of Pennsylvania's limited winery legislation. The bill passed in 1968, and Presque Isle Wine Cellars and Penn-Shore Vineyards, also in North East, became Pennsylvania's first limited wineries when they opened in the spring of 1970.

Markko Vineyard

During the harvest seasons of 1967 and 1968, Arnulf Esterer took time off from his job as an industrial engineer to volunteer his services to Dr. Frank. Convinced that he could grow the vinifera in Ohio, Arnie (1, 3) established Markko Vineyard in 1969 in partnership with Thomas Hubbard. The small winery near Conneaut, Ohio (2), is known for its oak-aged wines, and Arnie continues experimenting with rootstocks and a variety of viticultural techniques.

White Mountain Vineyards

Growing grapes in New Hampshire is a challenge that John and Lucille Canepa (1) have conquered. They moved to Laconia on the shores of Lake Winnipesaukee in New Hampshire's lake country in 1958 and spent seven years studying viticultural techniques and planning their vineyard before planting grapes in 1965. They opened New Hampshire's only winery, White Mountain Vineyards (2), in 1969. While the vineyards and winery were both successful, years of struggling with the highly restrictive New Hampshire state monopoly system were to follow. New legislation passed in 1981 permits them to sell directly to restaurants and private wine stores in addition to the state-owned stores.

Frederick S. Johnson Vineyards

As an expert in tropical agricultural development, Frederick S. Johnson has been associated with large scale agri-business enterprises in many areas of the world. In 1960, he turned his attention to the 125 acres of Concord grapes growing on the family farm near Westfield, New York in the Chautauqua grape belt (1). He realized that opening a winery would be a way of maximizing the return from his vineyards and then proceeded to replace most of the Concords with French hybrid varieties. The winery (2) was built in 1961, and in recent years Bill Gulvin, on the right (3), has joined Fred as the winemaker.

Tabor Hill Vineyard

While the large wineries in Michigan have been in existence for many years, the first of the small premium wineries to open was Tabor Hill Vineyard in Buchanan, Michigan, established in 1972 (1). The original grape plantings were made by Leonard Olsen (2) and for the first few years, the business was run exclusively by Len and his family. Today, the business is incorporated and controlled by the Chi Company. One of the winery's highlights came in 1974 when two Tabor Hill wines, a Baco Noir and a hybrid Trebbiano, were selected to be served at a White House state dinner given by President Gerald R. Ford.

Chicama Vineyards

After making a study of temperature and climate on Martha's Vineyard, an island in the Atlantic Ocean ten miles south of Cape Cod, George (3) and Cathy Mathiesen planted their first five acres of vinifera grapes in 1971. Today there are 36 acres planted at Chicama Vineyards. Chicama, pronounced with a long "a," was the name of an Indian trail bordering their property. The winery (1, 2) was licensed in 1973 and became a farm winery in 1976. Two of the Mathiesen's six children are involved full time at the winery; Michael is the vineyard manager and Lynn is responsible for the Sea Mist line of sparkling wines. Left to right (4) are Michael, Cathy, Lynn and George Mathiesen.

Hargrave Vineyard

Today, the eastern end of Long Island is the site of many new vineyard plantings and a number of new wineries in various stages of planning. Much of the interest in this area, some 85 miles east of New York City, can be attributed to the efforts of Alex Hargrave (2) and his wife Louisa. They planted their first grapes on the North Fork of the island in 1973 after an extensive nationwide search to find just the right place to establish a family farm where the vinifera could be grown. The Hargraves now have 55 acres of vineyards. Their winery was opened in 1976 and while the winery has a sales room (1), Hargrave Vineyard does not offer tastings to the public. A "V.I.P." room (3) is reserved for use on special occasions.

Meredyth Vineyards

An uncertain livestock market in 1971 convinced Archie Smith, Jr. (2), to consider other uses for his land at Stirling Farm in Middleburg, Virginia. The decision was made to plant grapes, and in 1972 vines were put in with the idea of later establishing a winery. When the winery (3) was opened in 1976, it was named after Archie's grandmother. As the enterprise grew, Archie and Dody Smith were joined by a son, Archie, III (1), who today serves as vice-president, winemaker and vineyard manager; and a daughter, Susan, who is marketing director.

3

The Newcomers

The success and rapid growth of the Eastern wine industry continues to attract new people to the world of wine. It is a rare month when the opening of at least one new winery is not announced. While the newcomers have the advantage of the accumulated expertise and experience of those who preceded them, there is no lessening of the amount of dedication and effort required to get a new winery off the ground.

Months, sometimes years, of planning are a crucial first step in bringing a new winery into existence. The right site must be found, finances worked out, a supply of grapes assured, and numerous regulations compiled with. Also important are decisions on equipment, winery design, product line and marketing.

Eventually all is in readiness. Construction is completed, the initial vintage is made and bottled, and the long-awaited day arrives when the cash register rings up the first sale of wine to the public.

It will take still another year or two before the winery's name becomes known, a regular customer list is developed, sales are built up, and final touches are put on the winery. Only then does the newcomer become an established part of the Eastern wine scene.

The first visible sign that a winery is on the way comes when the physical plant is readied — whether it be the remodeling of an existing structure or building an entirely new one. Even then, much remains to be done, as Tom McKeon (1) seems to be thinking during the ground-breaking ceremonies for Brandywine Vineyards in New London, Pennsylvania.

Typical of the newest wineries in the East are Good Harbor Vineyards (2) in Lake Leelanau, Michigan, Chadwick Bay Wine Company (4) in Fredonia, New York, and Allegro Vineyards (3) in Brogue, Pennsylvania. Wineries frequently open in close proximity to one another, as was the case in the summer of 1982 when two Finger Lakes wineries, Plane's Cayuga Vineyard (6) and Wickham Vineyards (5), opened their doors within a few miles of each other.

From time to time a new winery will be opened with a familiar face at the helm. When Hermann J. Wiemer Vineyard opened in 1980 in Dundee, New York, it was the realization of a long term goal for proprietor Hermann Wiemer (2), a graduate of Geisenheim Institute in Germany. For many years Hermann served as winemaker for Walter Taylor at Bully Hill Vineyards in Hammondsport, New York, and also ran his own nursery specializing in grafted vinifera vines.

Another "old-timer" who recently saw the dream of opening his own winery come true is Eric Miller (1) of Chadds Ford, Pennsylvania. Eric spent eight years as winemaker and vineyard manager for his family's Benmarl Vineyards in the Hudson Valley, and another two years at Chadwick Bay Wine Company in Fredonia, New York, before joining his wife Lee Miller in establishing the Chadds Ford Winery in 1982.

A Wine Tour of the East

A wine region cannot be shown simply in terms of its extremes. By far the largest number of wineries fall comfortably between the biggest and smallest, the youngest and oldest. Included in this large and diverse group are some of the best known Eastern wineries.

Another way of looking at the wineries of the East is by their geographic location. Through such factors as climate, history, political boundaries, and the new viticultural area appellations, specific areas such as the Finger Lakes of New York are recognized as distinct wine districts. Even in those parts of the East with a much shorter history of grape growing (and where district identity still lies in the future), descriptive terms such as "the West Virginia wine industry" are in common use.

The informal wine tour that follows highlights what is happening in many different parts of the East today. Representative wineries have been chosen to illustrate each of the areas.

New England

The moderating influence of the Atlantic Ocean on the sometimes harsh New England climate is one reason why half of New England's wineries have been established along the coast from Connecticut to Boston. David Tower (1) chose to locate Commonwealth Winery (3) in Plymouth, Massachusetts, where the winery would be close to the Massachusetts vineyards.

Site selection has been an important factor in determining the location of wineries away from the coast. Textile executive Sherman Haight (2) found a favorable micro-climate outside Litchfield in the northwest corner of Connecticut for his winery, Haight Vineyard (4).

New York: The Hudson River Valley

As the oldest of New York's major grape growing areas, the Hudson River Valley can trace its wine history back to 1677. Vineyards and wineries can be found on both sides of the river from the Palisades just north of Manhattan to the mid-Hudson north of Poughkeepsie. Graphic designer Ben Feder (3) and his wife Kathy own Clinton Vineyards (1), not far from the small town of Clinton Corners on the east side of the river. They specialize in white wines, primarily Seyval Blanc, and recently added a Seyval Blanc champagne to their product line. In the nearby town of Amenia, novelist William Wetmore and his wife Margaret (4) operate Cascade Mountain Vineyards (2).

New York: The Finger Lakes

More than 30 wineries are to be found in the Finger Lakes, perhaps the best known wine district in the East. The wine industry centers around four of the long narrow lakes — Cayuga, Seneca, Keuka and Canandaigua — and extensive vineyards are planted around each. Overlooking the west branch of Lake Keuka is Chateau Esperanza. The Greek revival stone mansion (1, 6) housing the winery was built in 1838 and is currently being restored by John and Sherry Lebeck (5). Near Dundee on Lake Seneca is Glenora Wine Cellars (7), founded in 1977 by a group of large growers in the Finger Lakes. The tasting room (2) overlooks the vineyards. Leaving a career in advertising, Peter Johnstone (4) joined forces with Naples grower John Ingale, Jr., to create Heron Hill Vineyards (3), a white-wine-only winery built on a hillside high above Lake Keuka north of Hammondsport.

New York: Chautauqua County

More than 20,000 acres of grapes are grown south of Lake Erie in New York's westernmost county. Chautauqua County is part of the Concord Grape Belt, and most of the grapes grown here go directly to nearby juice plants. Wineries came relatively late to this area, and the first farm wineries were started by families long involved in grape growing. The Merritt Estate Winery (2) in Forestville opened in 1976. James M. Merritt, whose signature appears on all Merritt labels, died before the winery opened. His son, Bill Merritt (4, right) then became president of the winery. Other family members are involved, including Bill's wife Christi and his mother, Peggy Sample (4, left). A few miles away near Dunkirk, Gary Woodbury (3) and his sister-in-law, Page Woodbury, have established Woodbury Vineyards (1). Gary was an early grower of vinifera, planting them on the family fruit farm in 1967.

Ontario

Sandwiched between Lake Ontario and Lake Erie west of Niagara Falls is an area known as the Niagara peninsula. Most of Canada's large wineries are located here, supplied by the more than 20,000 acres of grapes grown on the peninsula. Inniskillin Wines (2) in Niagara-on-the-Lake was the first of Ontario's farm wineries to receive a license in modern times. After opening the winery in 1974, Don Ziraldo (1) supervised a period of rapid growth during which production at the winery increased to 200,000 gallons a year. Increasing in importance as a growing area today is an area in southwestern Ontario along the northern shore of Lake Erie not far from Windsor. Charal Winery and Vineyard in Blenheim is owned by Charlotte and Alan Eastman (3), who grow 160 acres of grapes at their Eastman Fruit Farms. When their winery opened in 1977, it was the second to be licensed in the last 50 years in Ontario. Production at the winery is nearing 60,000 gallons, some of which is sold at the tasting room in a building along the highway that also houses the fruit market (4).

Pennsylvania: Lake Erie Area

Thousands of acres of grapes surround the small town of North East in Erie County, the center of the wine industry in northwestern Pennsylvania. As part of the Concord Grape Belt, the area has much in common with western New York State and eastern Ohio, so much so that the wineries along Lake Erie in the three states have applied for a multi-state viticultural area appellation stretching from Buffalo to Cleveland. Penn-Shore Vineyards (3) was one of the first two limited wineries to open in Pennsylvania in 1970, and was founded by three Erie County growers, Blair McCord, George Luke (4), and George Sceiford. Mazza Vineyards, with its Mediterranean-style architecture (2), opened in 1974. Bob and Frank Mazza (1) built the 50,000 gallon winery and six years later, in 1980, joined Charles J. Romito in a joint venture to operate both Mazza Vineyards in North East and Mount Hope Estate and Winery in Cornwall, Pennsylvania.

Pennsylvania: Southeast

With the exception of the wineries along Lake Erie and the Lapic Winery in New Brighton just north of Pittsburgh, the remainder of Pennsylvania's wineries are located in southeastern Pennsylvania in an area roughly bounded by State College on the west, Gettysburg and York to the south, and Philadelphia in the east. Favorable soil conditions and a moderate climate have led to the establishment of more than 25 wineries here.

Jerry and Kathy Forest (1) planted their first grapes in 1966 in Bucks County, north and east of Philadelphia, and opened their winery, Buckingham Valley Vineyards, in 1974. Today they have 15-1/2 acres of grapes and their suburban home (2) has required the addition of three wings to accommodate the expanding winery. Naylor Wine Cellars, located near Stewartstown in southern York County, was opened in 1978 by Dick Naylor (3) and his wife Audrey. The original cement block winery building is being replaced by a modern facility (4) with 40,000 gallons capacity. Nissley Vineyards (5), in western Lancaster County, was started in 1977 by Dick Nissley after he retired from his bridge construction firm. Dick, his wife Anna Ruth, and their four children are actively involved in managing the 35,000 gallon winery and its 28 acres of grapes.

Maryland

Those who grow grapes and make wine in Maryland must contend with a variety of climates and local option laws. When Bret and Sharon Byrd (4) opened their winery (1) in 1976, they found that their site ten miles west of Frederick was in a dry election district in a wet county, and they were allowed to open under the condition that they sell no wine in the district and drink none of their production themselves. In 1977 they were allowed to sell one bottle per brand per person per year to anyone taking a guided tour of the winery. It was not until 1978 that unlimited sales were permitted them on any day of the week. As in many other states, patience and perseverance paid off, and today Byrd Vineyards produces 12,000 gallons of wine a year, 60% of it sold at the winery.

Local laws were one of the obstacles confronting Philip and Jocelyn Wagner in 1945 when they opened Boordy Vineyards in Baltimore County. When they sold the winery in 1980 to the Deford family in Hydes, also in Baltimore County, the laws were still restrictive. Robert B. Deford, III (3), president and general manager of Boordy Vineyards, cannot sell at the winery without a second license, and the winery's 16,000 gallon production is sold through distributors. The winery (2) is located in a former dairy barn on the family farm.

New Jersey

Although there will soon be farm wineries in New Jersey as the result of recent legislation designed to encourage grape growing in New Jersey, all of the older wineries in the state hold what is known as a plenary winery license. The small winery that grows its own grapes will find it advantageous to hold a farm winery license; the holder of a plenary winery license will continue to have the freedom to buy grapes grown outside the state.

In Delran, north of Cherry Hill in western New Jersey, is Antuzzi's Winery. The winery (1), founded in 1974, has a capacity of 20,000 gallons. The owner, Matthew J. Antuzzi (3), has seen the demand for his strawberry wine soar to unexpected heights, reflecting the increased consumer interest in high quality fruit wines in eastern Pennsylvania and western New Jersey.

In the rolling hills of northern New Jersey almost due east of Easton, Pennsylvania, Dr. Daniel Vernon, Jr., divides his time between his veterinary practice and Tewksbury Wine Cellars. Founded in 1979, the winery (2) produces 14,000 gallons a year. The ability to buy out-of-state grapes made it possible to open the winery before the 20 acres of grapes come into full production in 1983.

New Jersey: Older and Larger

Not far from Atlantic City are several larger wineries that have played their part in giving New Jersey its tenth place ranking on the list of wine producing states. The two wineries closest to the resort city and its casinos have developed a profitable tourist business, particularly on rainy days.

The Renault Winery, to the west of Atlantic City in Egg Harbor City, is the oldest of New Jersey's wineries, having been founded in 1864 and in continuous operation since 1868. Champagnes and sparkling wines account for nearly half of the winery's production of 100,000 gallons, and a blueberry champagne is rapidly becoming the best selling wine. Joseph P. Milza (1), the present owner, has done much to refurbish both the interior and exterior (3) of the winery.

Gross' Highland Winery, located north of Atlantic City in Absecon, was founded in 1934 by John Gross and is currently owned by his grandson, Bernard F. "Skip" D'Arcy. Visitors to the 85,000 gallon winery (2) can take a self-guided tour aided by a slide presentation and information tapes. Also unusual is a self-service tasting room where vistors may pour their own samples. Wines are sold both at the winery and at an outlet in Manasquan.

Virginia

Although the number of acres of grapes planted in Virginia is relatively small, the number of wineries in Virginia has more than tripled in a few years. Some of the most liberal farm winery laws in the nation aided in this expansion. 21 wineries are located in all parts of the state, and it is yet too early to tell which areas may become established wine districts.

Shenandoah Vineyards (1) of Edinburg, licensed in 1977, became nationally known in 1981 when both the Shenandoah Valley of Virginia and the Shenandoah Valley of California sought to be approved as a viticultural area by the Bureau of Alcohol, Tobacco and Firearms. The winery produces 10,000 gallons of wine. Winemaker Alan Kinne, shown on the right with owners Jim and Emma Randal (2), also serves as general manager.

The Ingleside Plantation Winery is located in Oak Grove south of the Potomac River. Vines were first planted at the Flemer family's nursery in 1960, and the winery (4), opened in 1980. Current production is 13,000 gallons. Doug Flemer serves as vice-president, and Jacques Recht (3), for many years a professor of enology and technology at the National Fermentation Institute of Brussels, is the winemaker.

Virginia: European Ventures

Establishing a vineyard and opening a winery require a great deal of money. Most Eastern wineries have depended on the owner's financial resources plus his borrowing power, and to date there has been little investment in wineries or vineyards from outside the East. Two of the wineries in Virginia, however, are controlled by European interests.

Barboursville Vineyards is owned by Zonin S.P.A., of Gambellara, Italy. An 850-acre farm was bought in Barboursville in 1976, and the first 28 of a planned 250 acres of vinifera (3) have now been planted. The first wines were made in 1980. The three Zonin brothers who control the parent winery closely follow the operations in Virginia. Gaetano Zonin, is shown here with his wife Maria Theresa (4) in the interior of the winery.

In 1978, Dr. Gerhard W. R. Guth, a surgeon from Hamburg, Germany, planted the first grapes on a 2,000-acre farm he had purchased south of Culpeper. Today, 25 acres of a projected 250 acres have been planted, and the first wines from Rapidan River Vineyards (2) were placed on sale in 1981. Geisenheim-trained Joachim C. Hollerith (1) serves as vineyard manager and winemaker.

The Southeast

The southeastern states have their own unique native grapes, the Scuppernong and its close relatives, the muscadines. In 1524, the explorer Verrazano reported seeing them in the vicinity of Cape Fear, North Carolina, and British admiral John Hawkins noted in 1565 that the French at Fort Caroline in Florida had made 20 hogsheads of muscadine wines. Wines made from these grapes have won a devoted following; during the 20 years preceding Prohibition, Captain Paul Garrett's Scuppernong blends marketed under the name Virginia Dare were the best selling wines in the United States.

Duplin Wine Cellars in Rose Hill, North Carolina, makes wine exclusively from these native grapes. The winery (2), a growers' cooperative, opened in 1975. Production has grown from 3,000 gallons in 1975 to 80,000 in 1981. David Fussell (1) is the winemaker. Among the wines he makes is the only 100% Scuppernong wine now available.

In Lake City, South Carolina, Dr. James Truluck (4) and his son Jay operate Truluck Vineyards. The 20,000 gallon winery (3) is built in the style of a small French chateau winery. Most of the wines are made from French hybrids, although muscadines and vinifera are also used.

Northern Ohio

The escarpment that borders the southern shore of Lake Erie in New York and Pennsylvania gradually comes to an end in eastern Ohio. Growers in northern Ohio must rely on favorable microclimates in areas where the escarpment fails to provide protection against late spring and early fall frosts. Farther west, in the Sandusky area, grapes are grown on the offshore islands, a peninsula, and an area on the mainland near Sandusky Bay.

East of Cleveland, near the town of Madison, the Debevc family has extensive plantings of grapes. Their winery, Chalet Debonné Vineyards (2), has production facilities underground and a tasting and sales room on the ground floor of the chalet. Since Ohio has fewer restrictions than many other states, the Debevcs are able to operate a restaurant and, in addition, sell wine for consumption on the premises. Tony Debevc (1), president and winemaker, has long been active in the Ohio Wine Producers Association.

The Grand River Wine Company is also located near Madison. Bill Worthy (4) planted vineyards in 1972, sold grapes to area wineries for several years, and opened his own winery in 1978. The tasting room is located in a ranch style house (3), and a covered area nearby is used for weddings and other special events.

Southern Ohio & West Virginia

While the climate in southern Ohio is moderate, sharp winter temperature drops and late spring frosts concern growers in that part of the state. The oldest grape growing area is in the southwestern part of Ohio, and the majority of the grapes in southern Ohio are grown there today. Southeastern Ohio has fewer vineyards, and the climate is similar to that found to the east in the northern grape growing section of neighboring West Virginia. Selecting favorable micro-climates is of the utmost importance in both areas. A second wine district in West Virginia is located to the south near Charleston where there are approximately 1,000 more degree days during the growing season.

In 1969, Ken and Jim Schuchter planted 20 acres of French hybrids northwest of Cincinnati, in Morrow, as the first step in establishing their winery, Valley Vineyards. Today they have 45 acres of grapes, and the winery (2) produces 30,000 gallons a year. Late spring frosts are guarded against through the use of a helicopter to keep air moving when temperatures start to drop. The winery holds a festival at the end of each September, and more than 75,000 people attend, coming from as far away as Chicago.

A farm winery bill finally become law in West Virginia in 1981. The West Virginia Grape Growers Association led by Bob Pliska (left, 1), executive secretary, and Kurt Rauscher, president, lobbied for its passage. The first winery to open in West Virginia was Fisher Ridge Wine Co., north of Charleston in Liberty. The West-Whitehill Winery opened in Keyser in 1982, and Bob Pliska plans to open his own winery in late 1982.

Michigan

The traditional grape growing area of Michigan borders Lake Michigan north of the Indiana line, and most of the older and larger wineries are located there in the general vicinity of Paw Paw. They have been joined in recent years by a number of smaller wineries. Fenn Valley Vineyards, three miles south of Fennville, is run by William Welsch and members of his family. Doug Welsch (2) serves as winemaker for the family's 50,000 gallon winery (1, 4) and supervises the care of the vineyards. More than 50 of an eventual 100 acres of grapes have now been planted.

200 miles to the north is the Grand Traverse Bay area of Michigan, the state's newest wine district. The largest of the wineries, Leelanau Wine Cellars, located in Omena on the Leelanau Peninsula, is owned by several of the area's large fruit growers. Over one-third of the winery's production of 37,000 gallons is sold at the main tasting room in Traverse City (5) and a second tasting room in the tourist town of Frankenmuth (3). Both tasting rooms are located at the site of branch wineries.

The Upper Midwest

Apart from the long-established wine industry in Michigan, the upper Midwest is an area with a future rather than a past. Several wineries in Illinois are expected to open following passage of a long-awaited farm winery bill. With the exception of the Wollersheim Winery, most of the wineries in Wisconsin and Iowa are specializing in fruit wines. In Minnesota, a determined group of growers annually contends with the difficult winters in that state. Currently there are a half dozen wineries in Indiana.

The larger of Minnesota's two wineries is Alexis Bailly Vineyards in Hastings. Minneapolis attorney David Bailly and his daughter Nan (1) grow ten acres of grapes and produce 4,000 gallons of wine. Built entirely from Minnesota wood and stone, the winery building (2) was the first building in the state to be constructed as a winery.

The Golden Rain Tree Winery in Wadesville, Indiana, was opened in 1975 by a group of Indiana businessmen interested in finding a market for their grapes. They hired Dr. Murli Dharmadhikari (3) as their winemaker and built a 30,000 gallon winery and the Swiss chalet (4) that houses a restaurant. The winery gets its name from the oriental golden rain trees that grow at nearby St. Wendel.

Among the staunchest boosters of Indiana wines are Ben and Lee Sparks (5) who own Possum Trot Vineyards in Unionville. They have planted more than 30 acres of French hybrids, and their winery is housed in a century-old barn.

Missouri

Wine was first made in Missouri in 1823 by French Jesuit priests, and during the 19th century the state was an important center of viticulture and winemaking in the East. One of today's wine districts with an historic past is found along the Missouri River from Augusta to Hermann where grapes are planted on the river hills. A traditional grape growing area in Missouri is in the vicinity of St. James, about 100 miles southwest of St. Louis, where a plateau is the main geographic feature. While there are other districts in Missouri, one area that is receiving increased attention is the southwest corner of the state, west of Branson. Here the hillsides and temperate climate have attracted many new plantings.

Mount Pleasant Vineyards in Augusta stands on the site of a winery of the same name built in 1881 by a Lutheran minister, Friedrich Münch. Lucian and Eva Dressel opened their winery (1) in 1968, and they have maintained a link with the past by including on their wine list such historic wines as Münch and Cynthianna.

St. James Winery was opened in St. James in 1970 by industrial microbiologist Jim Hofherr and his wife Pat (3). About 50 of an eventual 90 acres of grapes have now been planted, and the winery (2) is the second largest domestic winery in the state with a production of 40,000 gallons.

Arkansas

Although grapes are grown and wine is made in various parts of Arkansas, the center of the state's wine industry is near Altus, a small town about 70 miles east of Fort Smith in the foothills of the Ozark Mountains. Among the early settlers in this area were Johann Andreas Wiederkehr from Switzerland and Jacob Post from Bavaria. Both arrived in 1880, grew grapes and started wineries that their descendants operate today.

The largest winery in Arkansas is Wiederkehr Wine Cellars, run by Alcuin Wiederkehr (1), Johann's grandson, who oversees the winery's 600 acres of grapes and the production of just over a million gallons of wine. The winery complex, located near the top of St. Mary's Mountain, is known as Wiederkehr Village and is designed in the style of an Alpine village. One of the attractions is the Weinkeller Restaurant (3, foreground). Wines are sold in Arkansas and adjoining states.

At the bottom of St. Mary's Mountain is the Post Winery (2). Mathew J. Post, great-grandson of Jacob Post, and nine of his twelve children tend 135 acres of grapes and make 200,000 gallons of wine. Most of the wines produced at Post are sold in Arkansas. Nearby is the smaller Mount Bethel Winery, run by Eugene J. Post, Mathew's brother.

South of Ohio

There are a half dozen wineries in Kentucky and Tennessee, all of them small and all of them founded in recent years. Legislation remains a basic need, and both the Kentucky Vineyard Society and the Tennessee Oenological and Viticultural Society are actively working to improve the climate for wineries in their respective states. Typical of the smaller wineries in these states is Tiegs Vineyards (5) in Lenoir City, not far from Knoxville. Terry Tiegs (4), a nuclear engineer in nearby Oak Ridge, his exwife Sue and brother Peter opened their winery in 1980 in the basement of Terry's home (6). Local option laws restrict marketing possibilities and the Tiegs' annual production of 1,250 gallons is sold at the winery and to Terry's fellow employees at Oak Ridge.

Wineries returned to Mississippi for the first time since Prohibition when the Mississippi Native Wine Law was passed in 1976. The Winery Rushing (2) was opened in Merigold by Sam and Diane Rushing (1) in 1977. All of their 15,000 gallons of wine is made from muscadines, and they grow three varieties in their 25-acre vineyard across the bayou from the winery. Manning the tasting room is Sam's grandfather, Big Tom Rushing (3), whose reputation for "busting" stills during Prohibition was immortalized in 1929 in a ballad, "The Tom Rushing Blues."

The Southwest

Winemaking in Texas and New Mexico goes back to the late 1600s when Franciscan priests brought the Mission grape into the El Paso area. The lone surviving winery of the many that existed before Prohibition is the Val Verde Winery located near the Rio Grande in Del Rio, Texas. Val Verde, celebrating its centennial in 1983, is now owned by the founder's grandson, Tom Qualia.

A feasibility study to determine the merit of growing grapes in Texas was completed at Texas A & M University in the early 1970s. This study, coupled with a number of years of practical experience, indicates that there will be at least six quite different areas in Texas where grapes can be grown. The south and east of Texas is hot and humid, suitable for growing native American varieties. In central and north central Texas the French hybrids have done well. The University of Texas has a vineyard project now totalling 320 acres in the southwestern part of the state. Another area receiving attention is the hill country to the south of Austin.

One of the pioneer growers in the north of Texas is Bobby Smith (2), a doctor in the Dallas-Fort Worth area who has 12 acres of grapes and a winery in Springtown. The winery, La Buena Vida Vineyards, was established in 1978 and now produces between 10,000 and 15,000 gallons of wine a year. Since Springtown is a dry area, Bobby opened a tasting room and separately bonded winery in Lakeside near Fort Worth in the summer of 1982.

The diversity of climates in New Mexico is as great as in Texas. Vineyards have been planted in very cold conditions at 9,000 feet altitude near Taos, and also near Las Cruces where the climate is hotter than Algeria and the growing season approaches 9,000 degree days. Rico's Winery (1) in Albuquerque was founded in 1947 by Enrico Gradi and was purchased by Tony Claiborne following Enrico Gradi's death in 1974. Tony, whose 6,000 gallon winery is one of the largest in the state, plans to move the winery to Bernalillo, 20 miles outside Albuquerque, in 1983.

From All Walks of Life

Part of the identity a winery acquires with the passage of time is linked to the people closest to it. These "connections" between people and wineries may be apparent in the winery structure or decor, in the types of wines for sale, in the labels, or in the marketing approach. Sometimes the link is an obvious carryover from an occupation or avocation. At other times it may be a reflection of a personality or a way of life. Wine people come from all walks of life, and each winery has its own individual stamp. Part of the understanding of Eastern wineries comes through discovering these individual stories.

Bucks Country Vineyards

Art Gerold (3) opened Bucks Country Winery (2) in New Hope, Pennsylvania, while he was president of Brooks-Van Horn Costume Company, one of the largest costume designers in New York City. His association with and love of the theater is apparent at the winery where the upper level has been turned into a fashion museum for the display of costumes worn by famous stage personalities. Broadway set designer Ben Edwards handled much of the winery's interior decor. Many of the winery's special events feature such well-known entertainers as José Greco. When Art opened his first extension of premises in Reading, Pennsylvania, he included a small wine museum in the tasting area (1).

At the end of the longest row I hang
The baskets on the end-post, a round shaft
Of cedar angled back for support and
Soaked in the dark smooth oils. I touch the craft
Of that wood and the vines, hardening toward
Winter, curve up and swing in the wind, and
Then I see you, bent, coming forward
Wire by wire in the limp green, your hand
Brushing the red wood from your face, inclined
And bobbing, a small smile, then your hand. Half
The day is gone, the tip of each leaf fined
To a gold-yellow in this light. I laugh
And think; How clumsy, how frail! The night's cold
Will end it! A bird sings and we are old.

Rose Bower Vineyard

Rose Bower Vineyard and Winery was opened in Hampden-Sidney, Virginia, in 1979 by poet Tom O'Grady (1) and his wife Bronwyn. Tom attempted to capture the love and romance of grape growing and winemaking through poetry, and this led to the making of a 30-minute motion picture about the vineyard and winery year as told through his poetry and the photography of Charlotte Schrader. The film, The Land is a Woman, premiered at the Albemarle Harvest Wine Festival in Charlottesville, Virginia, on October 17, 1981. The above poem is the final one in a sequence of 33 contained in a collection of his poetry entitled Establishing a Vineyard.

Lucas Winery

"Tug Boat White" is the name of one of the wines marketed by Bill and Ruth Lucas (3) whose Lucas Winery (1) was founded in 1980 in Interlaken, New York. Bill works in the vineyards and winery one week and then leaves to spend a week as captain of a tugboat owned by the Gulf Oil Corporation. The tugboat theme is carried out on the labels of two of the wines, Tug Boat White and Tug Boat Red, on T-shirts, and in a drawing of the tugboat made by a friend (2).

Boskydel Vineyard

Bernard C. Rink (1) is the founder of Boskydel Vineyard (2), located on a slope overlooking Lake Leelanau, Michigan. Bernie is also the librarian at Northwestern Michigan College. While his two careers may seem unrelated to an outsider, the marriage of books and wine is evident at Boskydel. One such example is the name of the winery itself. As Bernie tells it, with his typical sense of dry humor, "The name Boskydel came from an English professor I had who wrote stories for his kids called The Elves of Bosky Dingle. In these stories there were four little elves who lived under a stump in Bosky Dingle. In archaic English, that means Shady Glen. He died the year we built the winery, and I learned more from him than from any man except my father. I thought that somehow we would name the winery after the stories, and I put two words together, Bosky and Dell — I changed the Dingle to Dell. Then someone gave me a print that first year with Bosky Dell Road on it, and indeed there is a road down in southern Indiana with that name. We couldn't have that, so I knocked off one "l" and made it one word. And so we're now Boskydel." The "we" Bernie refers to so often includes the rest of his family, wife Suzanne and their five sons, who are very much involved in the winery's activities.

Adams County Winery

In 1967, Ronald F. Cooper (3) had gone as far as he could go in his career as an electronics engineer on Long Island, New York, without owning his own company. He looked at the crowded conditions on Long Island and decided on a simpler life in the country. Two career possibilities occurred to him: building harpsichords and making wine, for which he had won prizes as a home winemaker in his native England. Wine seemed to be an attractive, gentle way to make a living, and Ron and his wife Ruth (2) moved to Orrtanna, Pennsylvania where they opened Adams County Winery (1) in 1975. Although the vineyards and winery take most of their time (Ron remains a consultant in electronics) there is opportunity to pursue their love of music, Ruth's art and sculpture, and a myriad of Ron's interests from hybridizing cacti to building an occasional harpsichord or pipe organ.

Meier's Wine Cellars

Robert Gottesman (1) spent 21 years in sales for Schenley Distillers before leaving in 1957 to purchase Paramount Distillers in Cleveland, Ohio. As president of the distillery, Bob increased annual sales from 30,000 cases a year to more than a million cases today. Bob entered the wine business in 1976 when Paramount purchased Meier's Wine Cellars in Cincinnati following the death of Meier's owner, Henry O. Sonneman. In his first year as chief executive officer of Meier's, Bob turned a $750,000 loss the previous year into a profit. Acquisitions followed rapidly: North Bass Island in 1977 for its vineyards, the Lonz Winery on Middle Bass Island in 1979 and, a year later, both Mon Ami Champagne Company (2) and Mantey Vineyards (3) in the Sandusky area. The Gottesman way of doing business — tough and efficient, yet fair — is a trademark of each of his operations.

Sakonnet Vineyards

When Jim and Lolly Mitchell (3) decided to get married in 1973, Jim had a career background in energy and petrochemicals, and Lolly had been working in the field of public relations. Marriage meant a new life doing something together, and they hoped to combine a small business with land use and an art form. Through an intellectual process of elimination (second choice was a cheeserie), they decided on vineyards and eventually a winery. In 1975 they planted their first vines in Little Compton, Rhode Island, and in the same year received the license for their winery, Sakonnet Vineyards (1, 2). The hard work, dedication and success over the years has in one sense been a romantic adventure, a true life love story — both with wine and with each other.

Cedar Hill Wine Company

Like many men and women in the medical profession, Dr. Thomas Wykoff is a connoisseur of food and wine. Unlike most doctors, however, Tom has turned that love into a number of successful careers carried on simultaneously. In the medical field, he is an ear, nose and throat specialist: hospital department head, medical school professor, and private practitioner. As a restaurateur, Tom owns Au Provence, a Cleveland Heights, Ohio, restaurant that has won many prestigious awards for its cuisine classique, prepared by chef Richard Taylor (1). In the world of wine, Tom is the proprietor of both a retail store and a winery. The winery is the Cedar Hill Wine Company, opened in the basement of his restaurant in 1974. Like Tom's own busy life, the winery is full of constant activity, change and experimentation — and a touch of the unusual. Wines, for example, are marketed under the Chateau Lagniappe label, a name borrowed from New Orleans patois, where lagniappe stands for that "little bit extra," as in the thirteenth of a baker's dozen. Two familiar faces at the winery are Tom's wife Bev (2), shown here sharing a rare quiet moment with Tom, and cellarmaster Jack Foster (3).

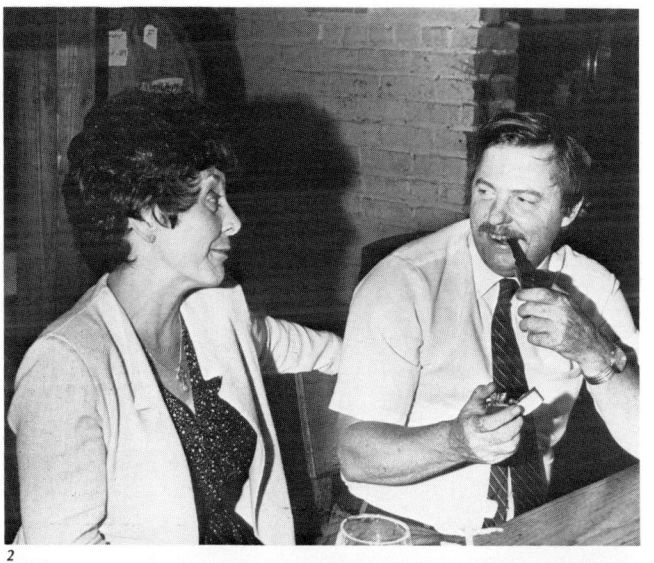

The East Today: The Supporting Cast

If the wineries, winemakers and growers occupy center stage on the Eastern wine scene, there are also those who help make it possible without attracting much public attention. The Eastern wine industry has its own supporting cast, who provide basic research and guidance, organize societies and conferences, write books and publish magazines, and sponsor competitions and tastings of the wines. While they may not be the visible "stars," they are important in their own right.

Included in the supporting cast are people like Bob Perna (2), owner of L'ecole de Vin, a wine school in Philadelphia, and Dr. Frank Gadek (1), a professor of chemistry at Allentown College who teaches winemaking. Growers seldom receive the recognition they deserve, but in Ontario each year the outstanding grower is honored as the Grape King. In 1981, Canada's Governor-General (right, 3) visited the vineyard of the king, Gary Pillitteri (behind driver on the mechanical harvester, 3).

Research & Extension Work

Basic and applied research have been responsible for much of the progress the Eastern wine industry has made to date. Major research stations have engaged in such extensive projects as development of new grape varieties and the modification of wine flavor components. Besides support on the "laboratory" level, there are experts in viticulture and enology who give practical advice in the field not only to those already engaged in the industry, but to those who would like to enter it.

The New York State Agricultural Research Station at Geneva, New York, celebrated its centennial in 1982. More than 46 varieties of grapes have been developed at the station, which is part of Cornell University's College of Agricultural and Life Sciences. The station has an annual budget of $9,000,000, and employs 68 scientists, several of whom work full time with grapes and wine. The Food Research Laboratory (1) is one of several buildings at the station. Dr. Nelson J. Shaulis (2) was responsible for the development of the mechanical grape harvester and the Geneva double curtain trellising system; following the retirement of Dr. Shaulis in 1979, Dr. Robert Pool (4) was placed in charge of viticulture. As head of the Department of Food Science and Technology until 1982, Dr. Willard B. Robinson (5) built a strong research team that includes Dr. Terry E. Acree (7), a specialist in flavor technology, and Dr. Leonard Mattick (3) whose work has concentrated on the reduction of acidity in wine. Don F. Splittstoesser (6) is currently the head of this department.

The Horticultural Research Institute of Ontario at Vineland, Ontario, has carried out an extensive research program in both viticulture and enology. The station works closely with the wine industry of Ontario in the development of new grapes and wines, and has provided leadership in the establishment of wine standards for the province. For many years, Oliver A. Bradt (1) was in charge of the grape breeding program at Vineland and the experimental vineyards. Since his retirement in 1979, the position has been held by Helen Fisher (4). Dr. Emil Andersen (3) has worked on infrared mapping of potential grape growing areas of the province to identify favorable micro-climates. Dr. Angus Adams (2) was head of wine research at Vineland from 1949 to 1981; among those who worked under him are Dr. Tibor Fuleki (5) developer of the Vineland Grape Flavor Index, and microbiologist Dr. Richard Chudyk (6), who developed a forecasting system for vineyard harvest dates. Dr. Chudyk also worked on the new Wine Quality Standards Program for Ontario wineries.

Some of the major state universities have scientists working with grapes and wine, both in research and extension work. Their activities are carried out primarily for the benefit of people in their home states. Typical projects include variety field testing to determine which grapes will grow best in different areas, and enological evaluation of wines made from those varieties. At Ohio State University, viticulturist Dr. Garth A. Cahoon (3, left) and enologist Dr. James F. Gallander (3) cooperate closely in working with the Ohio wine industry.

Three scientists function as a team at The Pennsylvania State University: viticulturist Dr. Carl W. Haeseler (4), enologist Dr. Robert B. Beelman (7), and entymologist Dr. Gerald L. Jubb, Jr. (2). Well-known scientists at other universities include Dr. Gordon S. Howell (6), Michigan State University; Dr. Bruce Zoecklein (1), University of Missouri; Dr. Daniel Carroll (5), North Carolina State University; and Dr. Richard P. Vine (8), Mississippi State University.

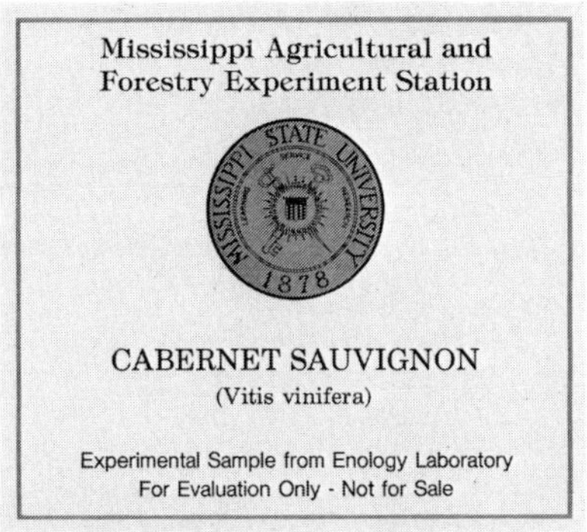

Mississippi Agricultural and Forestry Experiment Station

CABERNET SAUVIGNON
(Vitis vinifera)

Experimental Sample from Enology Laboratory
For Evaluation Only - Not for Sale

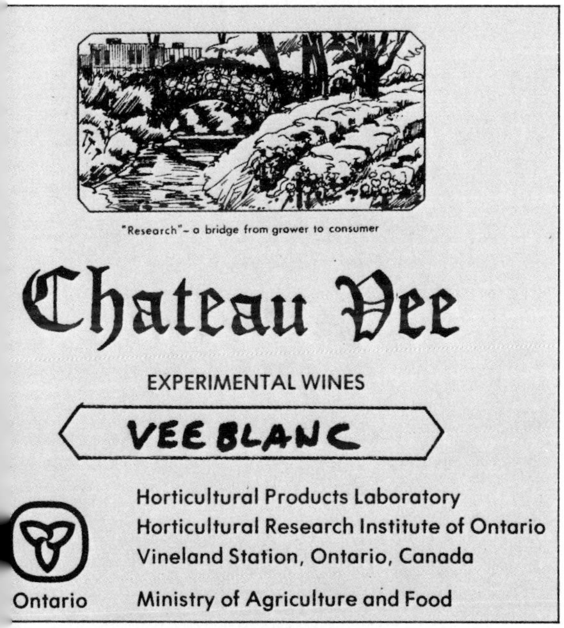

"Research" – a bridge from grower to consumer

Chateau Vee

EXPERIMENTAL WINES

VEE BLANC

Horticultural Products Laboratory
Horticultural Research Institute of Ontario
Vineland Station, Ontario, Canada

Ontario Ministry of Agriculture and Food

Geneva Cellars

Cayuga White

For Experimental Use

New York State Agricultural
Experiment Station, Geneva, New
York State College of Agriculture

A Statutory College of the State
University of New York at Cornell
University, Ithaca

The Nittany Lion Cellars

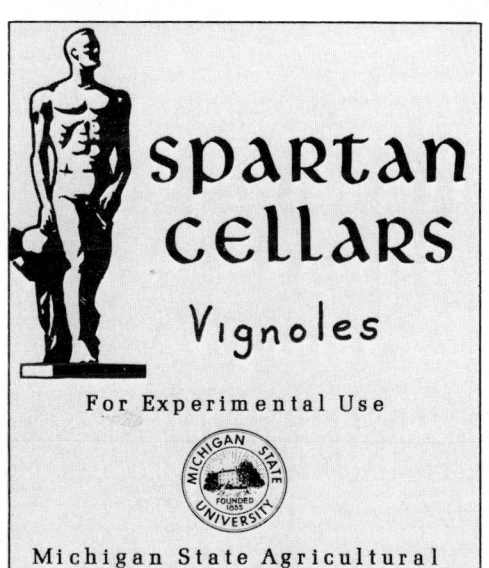

For experimental use only. College of Agriculture. The Pennsylvania State University

---

spartan cellars

Vignoles

For Experimental Use

Michigan State Agricultural
Experiment Station
East Lansing, Michigan

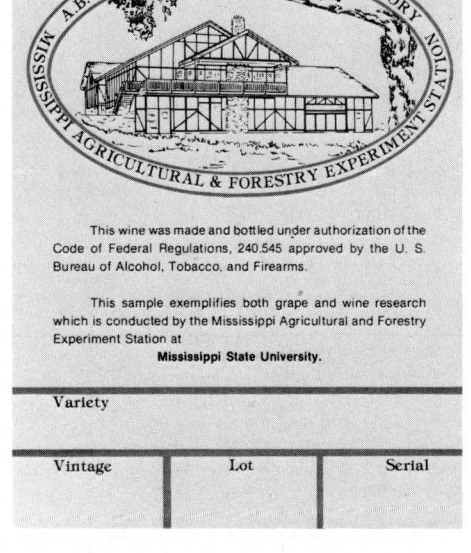

A.B. McKAY FOOD & ENOLOGY LABORATORY
MISSISSIPPI AGRICULTURAL & FORESTRY EXPERIMENT STATION

This wine was made and bottled under authorization of the Code of Federal Regulations, 240.545 approved by the U. S. Bureau of Alcohol, Tobacco, and Firearms.

This sample exemplifies both grape and wine research which is conducted by the Mississippi Agricultural and Forestry Experiment Station at **Mississippi State University.**

Variety			
Vintage	Lot		Serial

Wines produced at experimental wineries may not be sold, and there is no requirement that they even be labeled. However, in keeping with wine tradition, labels have been created for some of these wines.

The U.S. Department of Agriculture has research scientists around the country who are involved with grapes and wine. In the East, the best known is plant pathologist Dr. John McGrew (4), shown here receiving an award from the American Wine Society.

At a state level, extension agents work directly with the public and carry much of the responsibility of transmitting knowledge to growers and winemakers. Dr. Thomas J. Zabadal (1), here addressing a Virginia group on methods of bird control, is a New York State extension agent.

The East also has consultants in the private sector. Lucie T. Morton (2) of King George, Virginia, is active both in writing and lecturing. Her translation from the French of Pierre Galet's book on ampelography — grape vine identification — is the standard work available to Eastern growers today.

Although he is not associated with any university, Elmer Swenson (3) has worked for many years to develop winter-hardy grape varieties in his Wisconsin vineyard. The best known are Edelweiss and Swenson Red.

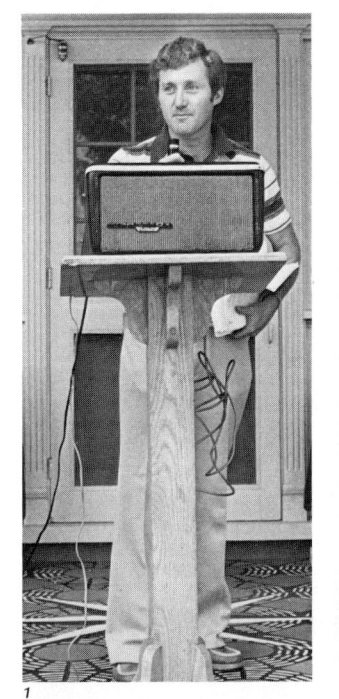

Conferences & Societies

People learn from each other, and in the East there are many ways people get together to acquire information, to become better informed and to share experiences. Conferences and societies are two important vehicles for this purpose. Societies range from those for professional winemakers to those for wine buffs who simply want to know more about their favorite subject. Conferences may be held by societies or they may be sponsored by state universities or private organizations. At some of these events there are wine competitions at which professional or amateur winemakers enter their wines not only for awards, but to see how their wines compare with those other winemakers have made.

The American Wine Society was founded in 1967 on Dr. Konstantin Frank's front porch by a group of home winemakers. From this simple beginning, the Society has grown to a membership of over 2,000, including professional and amateur winemakers, wine educators and wine lovers. Annual meetings give members the opportunity to taste wines (3) and listen to prominent speakers such as California's Leon D. Adams (2). Each year awards are given to those who have made outstanding contributions to American wine or to A.W.S.; in 1978 the outstanding member award was presented by then-president Kathryn Froelich to J. Edward Schmidt of Pennsylvania (1). Two prominent members of the Society are Philip and Margaret Jackisch of Royal Oak, Michigan (4). Margo Jackisch served as executive secretary of the Society for nine years and edits the quarterly journal.

The American Society of Enologists is a professional organization for those interested in the technical aspects of winemaking. In 1976, an Eastern Section of the Society was founded as a branch of the national organization. Winemakers and researchers gather each summer at the annual meeting to listen to technical papers (2) and exchange ideas. The Eastern Section maintains and funds a library resource center in Geneva, New York. Here Dr. Andrew C. Rice (1) of the Taylor Wine Company gives the annual library report. Another project of the Eastern Section is the administration of a scholarship fund for students of enology and/or viticulture, established by Wineries Unlimited, an Eastern trade conference. In 1981, Dr. Willard B. Robinson of the New York Agricultural Experiment Station presented a scholarship check to student Andy Reynolds (3).

Two other organizations that appeal to special groups are the Society of Wine Educators and the Vinifera Wine Growers Association. The S.W.E. is a national organization that holds its annual meetings in the East every second year. The V.W.G.A., headquartered in The Plains, Virginia, promotes the cause of growing vinifera in the East. The Association founded what has now become the Virginia Wine Festival and each year sponsors an annual seminar in conjunction with the festival.

The first president of the Society of Wine Educators, Robert J. Levine (2), of Princeton, New Jersey, was presented with an award in 1980 by wine writer Harriet Lembeck, as his wife Ginny looks on. S.W.E. members toured the Taylor Wine Company (1) during the annual meeting held at Cornell University in 1978. Senator John Warner of Virginia poured wine (3) into the Monteith Trophy being awarded to Elisabeth Furness of Piedmont Vineyards at the annual seminar of the V.W.G.A.

The largest trade conference in the East is Wineries Unlimited, sponsored by Eastern Grape Grower and Winery News, a trade magazine published in Watkins Glen, New York. Since 1976, those involved in the Eastern wine industry have been able once a year to attend seminars (3), get together with commercial exhibitors of winemaking equipment and supplies, and taste and critique each other's wines. Several weeks before Wineries Unlimited, the Eastern Wine Competition — the largest competition exclusively for Eastern wineries — is held in Watkins Glen. The award winning wines are announced at the closing night banquet at Wineries Unlimited. The Reverend Thomas Hayes (4), chief judge of the Competition, announced the winners in 1981. Robert Byloff (1) winemaker at Naylor Wine Cellars in Stewartstown, Pennsylvania, registered his pleasure at winning a medal, as did Alcuin Wiederkehr (2) of Wiederkehr Wine Cellars, Altus, Arkansas.

Tastings

One way to taste Eastern wines is to stop at a winery where visitors are encouraged to sample wines before making a purchase. Another way is to attend more structured tastings held by wine clubs or local chapters of wine societies. Throughout the East, tastings are arranged for different purposes, all intended to increase the taster's familiarity with the wines being served.

Many wine tastings are held on a "by invitation only" basis as part of the marketing process. Each spring, for example, members of Benmarl Wine Company's Société des Vignerons are invited to the winery to taste barrel samples of the wines to be bottled that year and to choose the ones they wish to have reserved for them. Volunteers, members of the family and employees pour wines at booths located throughout the winery; this tasting station (1) in the cellar of the winery was manned by Jack Schaller.

On a broader scale, the Association of American Vintners conducted back-to-back tastings at Windows on the World, a noted restaurant in New York City's World Trade Center. Participating wineries presented their wines first to the news media and then to New York retailers and restaurateurs. Among those showing their wines at Windows on the World were Jim and Lolly Mitchell (3) of Sakonnet Vineyards, Little Compton, Rhode Island. The seriousness of this tasting is evident in the attitude of the two men with Shorn Mills (2, right), general manager and winemaker at Haight Vineyards in Litchfield, Connecticut.

Wine tastings may be held for the dual purpose of raising money as well as introducing a public to wines. In March, 1979, nearly 1,000 people paid $15 apiece to taste a variety of wines at the Wooden Angel in Beaver Falls, Pennsylvania. Restaurant owner Alex Sebastian (4) turned over the restaurant for the day to the Upper Valley Jaycees for their annual fundraising event. One of those who volunteered his services for the affair was Ray Szymanski (3), president of the Pittsburgh chapter of Les Amis du Vin.

Each year at the Beacon Motor Inn in Jordan Harbour, Ontario, the Wine Council of Ontario sponsors a tasting of old, rare and limited edition Ontario wines in conjunction with the Niagara Grape and Wine Festival. In 1981, visitors were able to sample wines from Ontario wineries including Charal Winery & Vineyard (2) of Blenheim. Many members of the industry attended, including Dr. John Paroschy (1), a researcher with Brights Wines who spent the evening pouring his winery's limited bottling of Gewürztraminer.

Some wine tastings are held for educational purposes rather than sales. As a way of familiarizing Pennsylvania's legislators with the state's wine industry and its problems, the Pennsylvania Wine Association holds periodic tastings of Pennsylvania wines for members of the state legislature. Art Gerold (2) of Bucks Country Vineyards in New Hope, Pennsylvania, pours wine during one of these tastings.

In June, 1980, The Pennsylvania Grape Letter and Wine News sponsored a tasting for the specific purpose of evaluating old wines from the East. The results were later written up for publication. Discussing the aging potential of Eastern wines following the tasting were Eric Miller (1, left), of Chadds Ford Winery, and Dr. John McGrew, a scientist with the United States Department of Agriculture.

Fairs & Festivals

Take a large crowd, add music, entertainers, plenty of food and lots of wine, and the result is bound to be a festive occasion any time of year. Many wine festivals take place at harvest time, when the atmosphere becomes one of jovial celebration, setting the stage for the best known of all festival events — a grape stomping!

While festivals and fairs represent the "fun" side of wine, and everybody is expected to have a good time, there is a serious note to them as well. For the wineries involved, it means a chance to show off their wines and, most importantly, to sell them. Even when there is an admission charge, wine sales are necessary to help defray the many expenses of running a festival. Meredyth Vineyards of Middleburg, Virginia, holds a festival each May as a way of introducing their new vintage. Featured are a gourmet luncheon and an entertainment spectacular, in this case a bagpipe band (3) brought in from Washington for the day. Wine tasting is a major part of any festival, and Dick Naylor (2) of Naylor Wine Cellars in Stewartstown, Pennsylvania, appreciates a taste of his own wine as well as anyone else. Movies, vineyard tours and wine appreciation seminars are highlights of Naylor festivals. During the summer and early fall, festivals are a way of life at Mount Hope Estate and Winery in Cornwall, Pennsylvania. A different event is planned for every weekend: music of all kinds, a Renaissance Fair (1, 4), art shows, old car round-ups, a "Fifties" weekend, craft shows, and even authentic historical battle re-enactments.

The Niagara Grape and Wine Festival is the largest festival in Eastern North America, with the exception of the New Orleans Mardi Gras. More than 850,000 people come to the Niagara peninsula of Ontario to attend this ten-day event held late in September. The festival is designed to promote Ontario wines, and the 350 events held as part of the festival reflect the importance of grapes and wine to the area's economy. Parties, dances and balls creative a festive mood; wine bars are open daily, and winery and vineyard tours are offered at regular intervals. Special guests-of-honor serve as parade marshals, and "grape royalty" — king, queen and princess — make the rounds of most events, accompanied by Mr. and Mrs. Grape, the festival mascots. The largest single event is the Grande Parade, Canada's largest street parade.

120

Her Majesty Queen Bonnie
A Royal Welcome From
NIAGARA GRAPE & WINE
FESTIVAL

NIAGARA GRAPE & WINE
FESTIVAL QUEEN 1981

PANVIBES

What are these people watching? Answer: a good old-fashioned grape-stomping competition (1) — a sure-fire attention getter at any festival, including the one being filmed (2) at this Vinifera Wine Growers festival in Middleburg, Virginia.

The hot air balloon (3) owned by the Boar's Head Inn is readied for use during the Albemarle Harvest Wine Festival in Charlottesville, Virginia.

Publications

Chances are, anything you want to know about the Eastern wine industry can be found in print somewhere. In the East today, a wide variety of information — from the names and addresses of wineries, to the dates of festivals, to technical material on grape growing and winemaking — is available through winery newsletters, conference proceedings, state wine association brochures and a number of privately published journals and reference materials.

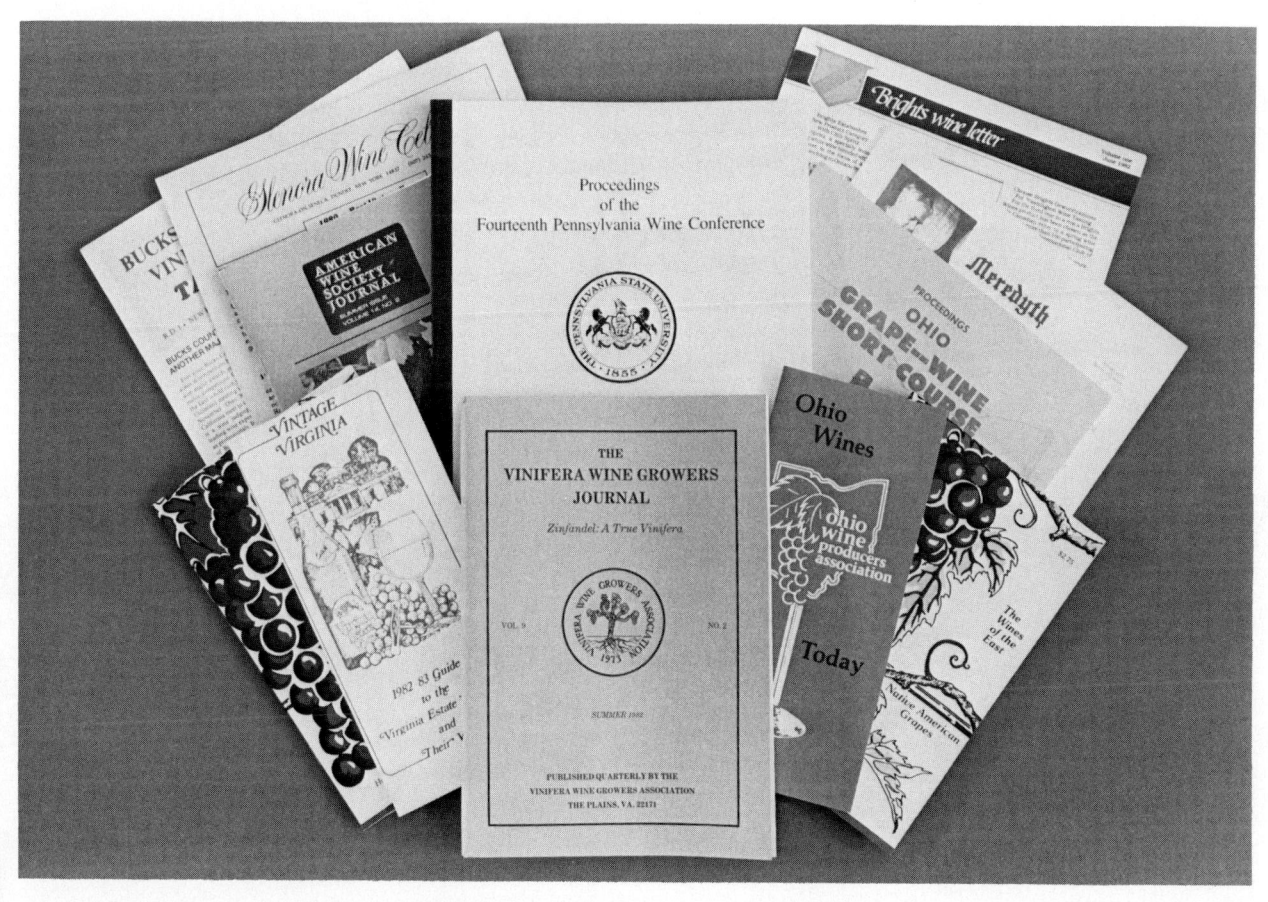

Resources for the Industry

Most industries have a trade magazine that publishes technical information and news about people in the industry. The trade magazine for the Eastern grape and wine industry is Eastern Grape Grower and Winery News (1), edited by Richard Figiel (5), and published in Watkins Glen, New York, by J. William Moffett (3) and Hope Merletti (4).

In addition to printing material of interest to growers and wineries, the magazine sponsors annual events for the trade such as a summer seminar in viticulture and, the week after Thanksgiving, a seminar and trade show called Wineries Unlimited (2). Bill Moffett also serves as administrative director for The Association of American Vintners, a trade association for Eastern wineries.

Telling the Story

The East has its own consumer wine magazine that helps to keep the public informed about the wines, people and events that make up the Eastern wine scene. Wine East (1) is edited by Hudson Cattell and is published in Lancaster, Pennsylvania, by L & H Photojournalism. Partner, publications manager and associate editor Linda Jones McKee (2, 4) works closely with art director Marian Broderick (2, right).

L & H Photojournalism also publishes a variety of informational publications about the East. A number of these have been co-authored by Hudson Cattell and Lee Miller (3), whose collaboration in writing about the Eastern wine industry goes back to the days when they co-edited The Pennsylvania Grape Letter and Wine News, the predecessor of Wine East.

The Wines
of the East

Perhaps the best way to understand the wines of the East is to become familiar with the grape varieties used. While at first glance there may appear to be an impossibly large number of them, many with strange or unfamiliar names, in reality only about a dozen varieties are in widespread use in all parts of the East.

On the facing page, the principal grapes used for winemaking are listed in three categories, each subdivided into whites and reds. The vinifera are a very old Asian species widely grown today in California and the classic wine regions of Europe. The native American grapes (including many species, but primarily *vitis labrusca*) are those that originated in North America. The hybrids are crosses whose parentage includes vinifera and native American grapes. One specific group of hybrids, called the French hybrids, are those that were originally hybridized in France and later brought to North America.

The wide variety of Eastern climates, soils and geography make some areas more suited to certain varieties than others. While many grape growers and wineries are still experimenting to find out which varieties will make the best wines in their area, the wines described on the following pages are those commonly made throughout the East, and which have attained consumer recognition.

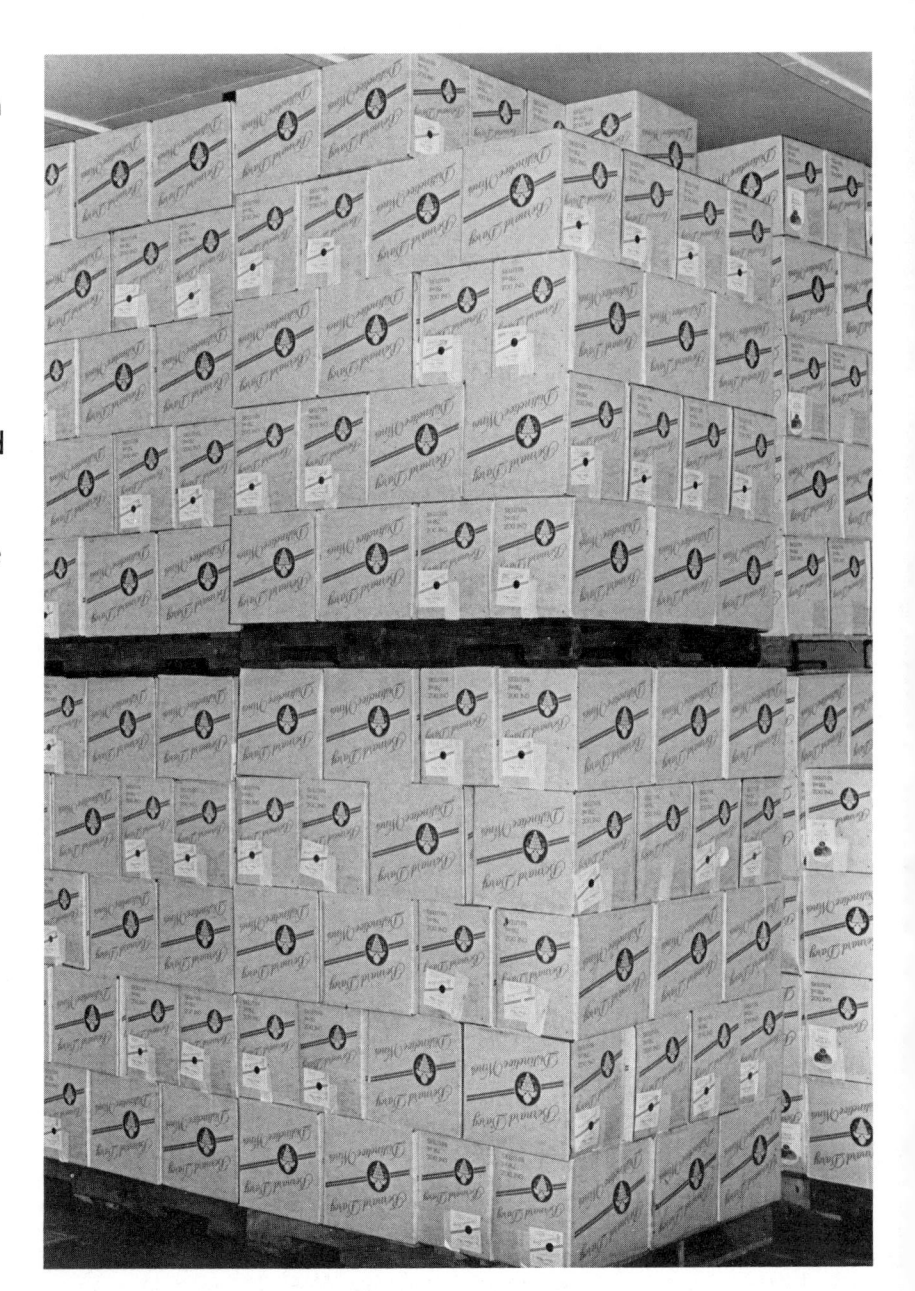

Some Eastern Grape Varieties

VINIFERA	NATIVE AMERICAN	HYBRIDS
White	*White*	*White*
Aligoté	Carlos	Aurore
Chardonnay	Catawba	Cayuga White
Gewürztraminer	Delaware	Edelweiss
Johannisberg	Diamond	Rayon d'Or
Riesling	Dutchess	Seyval Blanc
Sauvignon Blanc	Elvira	Seyve-Villard
Sémillon	Isabella	Verdelet
	Magnolia	Vidal Blanc
Red	Niagara	Vignoles (Ravat)
	Noah	Villard Blanc
Cabernet Sauvignon	Herbemont	
Gamay	President	*Red*
Merlot	Scuppernong	
Pinot Noir		Baco Noir
	Red	Beta
		Cascade
	Clinton	Chambourcin
	Concord	Chancellor
	Noble	Chelois
	Ives	DeChaunac
	Lenoir	Landal
	Steuben	Landot
	Worden	Léon Millot
		Maréchal Foch
		Rosette
		Rougeon
		Villard Noir

White Table Wines

There are more white table wines made in the East today than reds, reflecting the current consumer love affair with whites. As in other wine regions of the world, Eastern white wines range from very sweet to very dry, but often fall into these general categories:

1. Sweet and fruity
2. Fresh, fragrant and slightly sweet
3. Crisp, light and dry
4. Dry, medium-to-full bodied and complex, with some potential for aging

It is worth noting that some of the Eastern white varieties are used to make wine in more than one style. A good example is Seyval Blanc, which many wineries make in a young, fragrant, slightly sweet style, others as a more austere dry wine with prominant acidity, and still others as a rich, full-bodied, oak-aged wine. In some cases the same winery may produce two or three or more styles of Seyval Blanc.

In very broad terms — at the risk of oversimplification — the dry white table wines of the East more closely resemble the wines of France than those of California. In contrast, some of the East's best-known sweeter wines, which enjoy a wide following, are unique to the East in that they are made nowhere else in the world.

Seyval Blanc & Vidal Blanc

Seyval Blanc and Vidal Blanc are among the most recognized names of white wines in the East. Seyval Blanc is one of the oldest hybrid varieties to be planted extensively, while Vidal Blanc has risen to prominence only in the last five years. Both are used primarily for dry table wines, though they have a large following as slightly sweet wines as well.

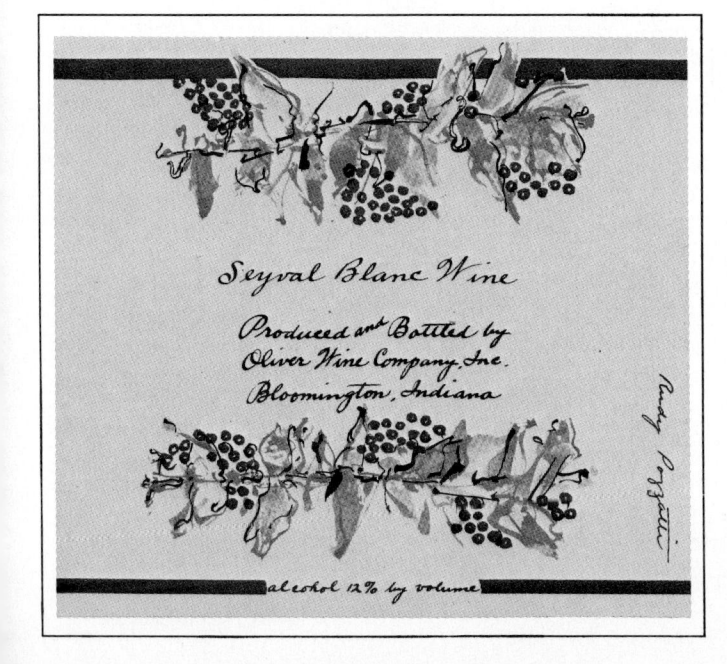

Chalet Debonné Vineyards
VIDAL BLANC
A Light Dry Table Wine
PRODUCED & BOTTLED BY CHALET DEBONNÉ VINEYARDS, INC.
MADISON, OHIO
ALCOHOL 12% BY VOLUME

St. James
Chill Well
Serve with light
Meat and Fish
Vidal Blanc
A Dry White Missouri grown table Wine
PRODUCED AND BOTTLED BY ST. JAMES WINERY · ST. JAMES, MO.
BONDED WINERY NO. 94

good harbor vineyards
1981 Michigan
Seyval Blanc
Produced and Bottled by
Good Harbor Vineyards
Lake Leelanau, Michigan 49653
BW-MI-49
Alcohol 11% by Volume

Seyval Blanc Wine
Produced and Bottled by
Oliver Wine Company, Inc.
Bloomington, Indiana
alcohol 12% by volume

Château des Charmes
Seyval Blanc
White Wine — Vin Blanc
11.5% alc./vol. — 750 ml
CHATEAU DES CHARMES WINES LTD., NIAGARA-ON-THE-LAKE, ONTARIO
PRODUCT OF CANADA — PRODUIT DU CANADA

Cayuga White

Cayuga White is the most recent of the East's white varietals, developed at the New York State Agricultural Experiment Station at Geneva in 1972. Generally fruity, and sometimes described as spicy, it is more often made semi-sweet than dry.

Aurore

Aurore (sometimes spelled Aurora) has been one of the most widely planted white grapes in the East. While many small wineries make Aurore as a varietal, it is often used as a blending grape by the larger wineries. For many people, Aurore has special appeal as a very young fruity wine.

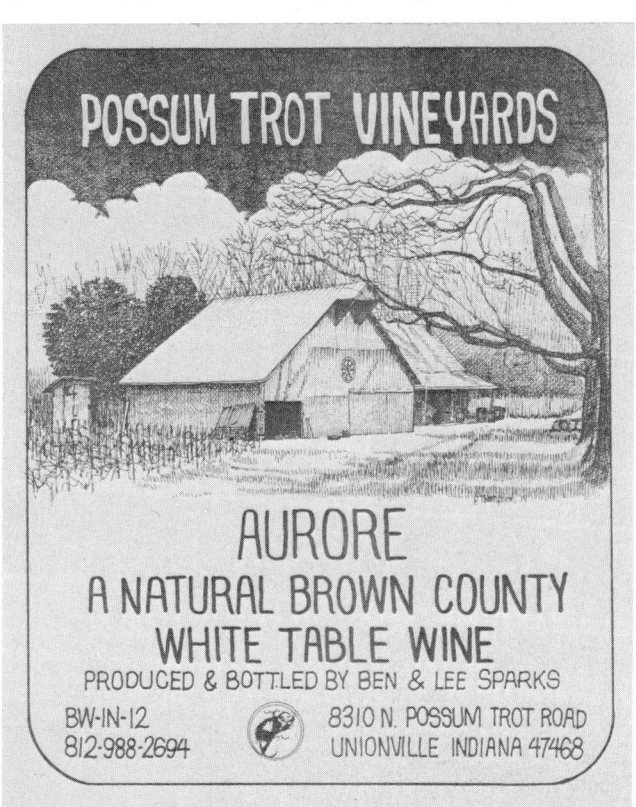

Catawba

Catawba is one of the best known of all the native American grape varieties. Powerful, musky, grapey, Catawba gained prominence as a sweet wine in the last century and its popularity continues unabated today.

Niagara

Niagara, with its prominent fresh grape taste, is a variety that is both gaining and losing favor in the East. Plantings are disappearing in Ontario, but are increasing sharply in other areas like southeastern Pennsylvania. It, too, is made almost exclusively as a sweet wine.

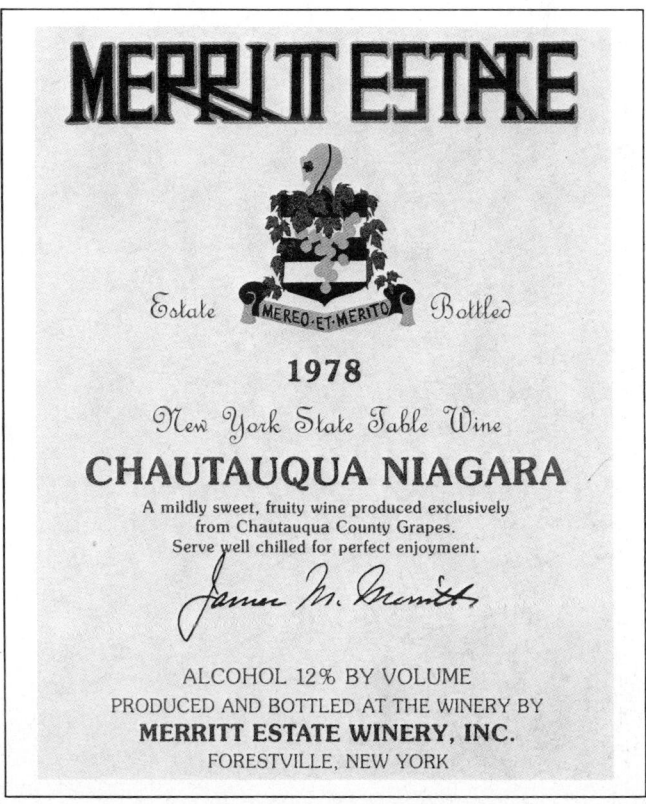

Dutchess

The subtle, delicate flavors of Dutchess contrast sharply with the forward, grapey qualities of wines like Niagara and Delaware. Sometimes described as smoky, Dutchess is made into a varietal wine with varying degrees of sweetness. It is also sufficiently full-bodied to use as a base for champagnes.

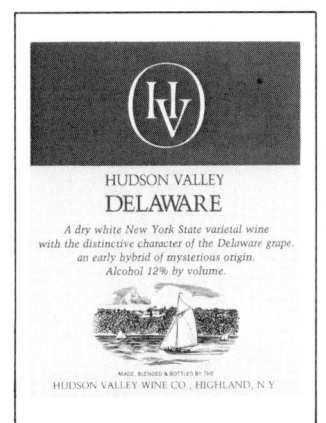

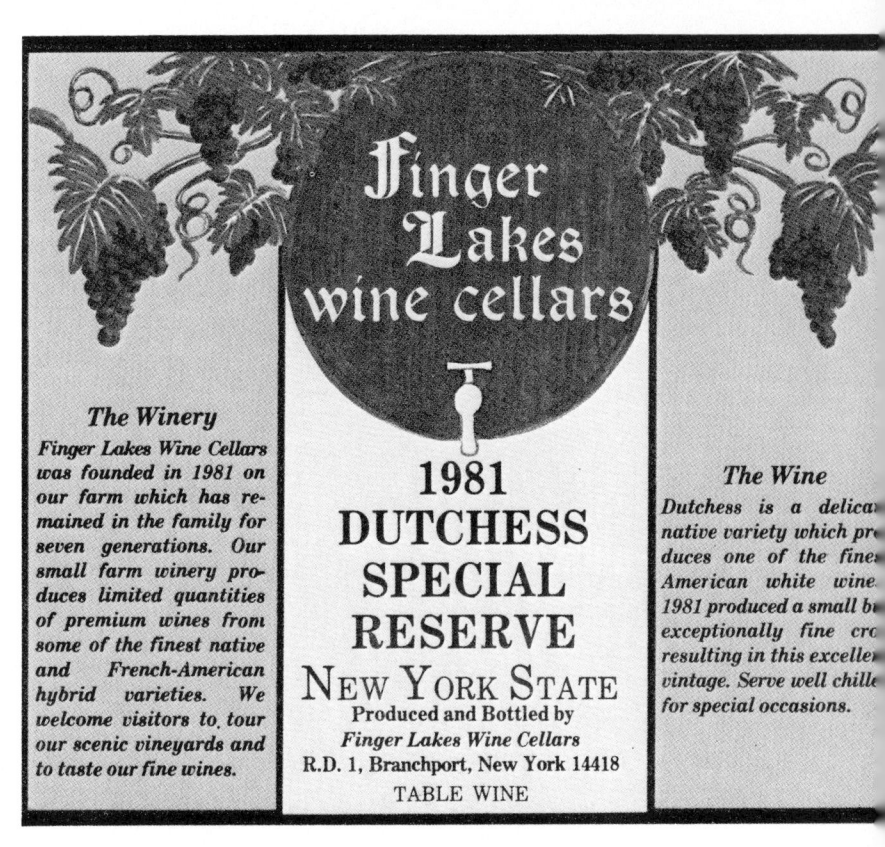

Delaware

Along with Concord, Niagara and Catawba, Delaware is one of the "big four" of the American varieties. Grapey, with a touch of mintiness, Delaware is made primarily as a sweet wine.

Chardonnay & Riesling

Chardonnay and Riesling are among the best known names in the wine drinking world. In the East, plantings of these two vinifera varieties are limited, and, as a consequence, production is small. Chardonnay and Riesling are recognized as two of the East's most prestigious wines, and command top prices in the marketplace.

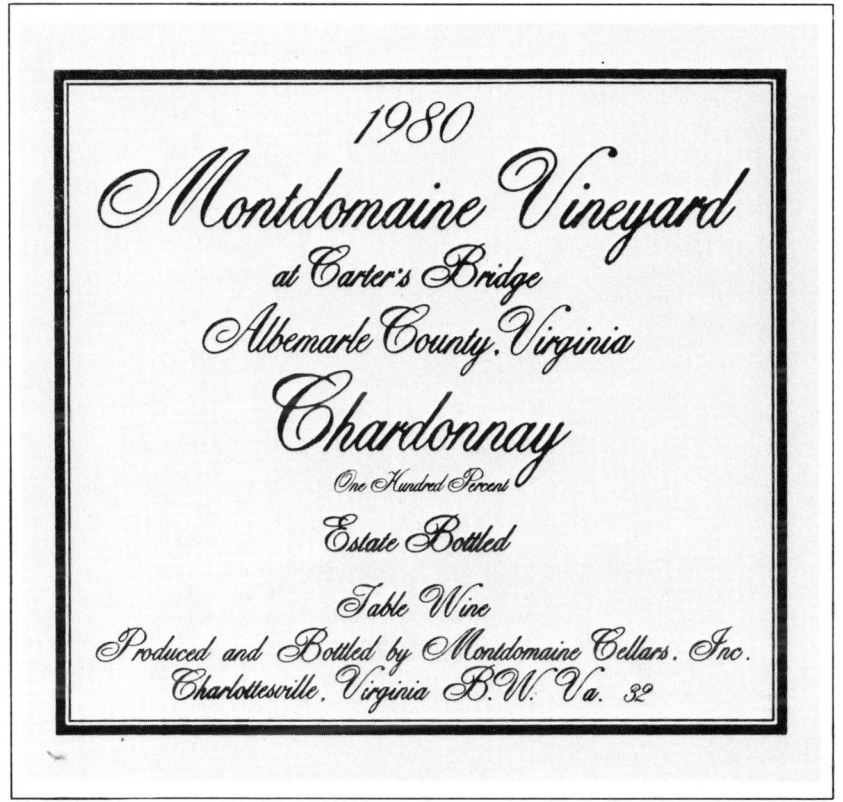

Piedmont Vineyards
Virginia Chardonnay
Merrill-Furness White Table Wine
PRODUCED AND BOTTLED BY
PIEDMONT VINEYARDS AND WINERY INC., MIDDLEBURG, VIRGINIA
ALCOHOL 12% BY VOLUME

1980
Montdomaine Vineyard
at Carter's Bridge
Albemarle County, Virginia
Chardonnay
One Hundred Percent
Estate Bottled
Table Wine
Produced and Bottled by Montdomaine Cellars, Inc.
Charlottesville, Virginia B.W. Va. 32

Wiederkehr
ARKANSAS MOUNTAIN
JOHANNISBERG RIESLING
1978
This pale gold, deliciously dry white table wine with pleasing tartness derived taste and fragrance from the rare Johannisberg Riesling grape, grown in our own mountain vineyards. Enjoy this all-purpose wine well chilled.
Produced and Bottled by Wiederkehr Wine Cellars, Inc. Altus, Arkansas. Alcohol 11% by Volume.
M-124 ATP

Fenn Valley
WHITE RIESLING
A WHITE TABLE WINE MADE 100%
FROM WHITE RIESLING GRAPES

This full bodied wine, produced from only the finest fully ripened Johannisberg Riesling Grapes, is made in the traditional German method and will continue to improve when aged in the bottle. FENN VALLEY White Riesling is a delicate and fruity wine of great bouquet which may be enjoyed by itself or with cheese, fowl, fish, seafood, veal, or pork delicatessen specialties. Best served slightly chilled (50-55°F).

PRODUCED AND BOTTLED IN THE NATURALLY COOL CELLARS OF
FENN VALLEY VINEYARDS • FENNVILLE, MICHIGAN 49408
11½% ALCOHOL BY VOLUME

Other Whites

Ravat, also known as Vignoles, is a white hybrid known for its fragrant, fruity characteristics. Wines made from this variety are presently found primarily in New York and Michigan, but its popularity is on the increase elsewhere. Gewürztraminer is a spicy, Germanic-like wine. As one of the least winter hardy varieties in the East, it is grown and made sparingly. Many wineries are now experimenting with Sauvignon Blanc, but at present the largest number of wines made from this variety can be found in Virginia. Canada Muscat and Couderc Muscat are two white hybrids used in the East to add a touch of muscat flavor to a wine.

Red Table Wines

The red wines of the East have been undergoing a quiet but significant period of change in recent years. In the past, most Eastern red wines were made out of the Concords and their relatives. While these sweet, grapey wines remain popular today, more and more Eastern wineries have added dry red table wines to their product lines.

The majority of today's dry reds fall into two categories: light, fresh, Beaujolais types for early consumption; and medium-bodied, berry-like wines that may continue to improve over a period of a few years.

More recently, a small but growing number of Eastern wineries have been attracting attention for their full-bodied, tannic reds with longer aging potential. The number of such wines is still limited because the production of reds for laying down is largely an uncharted territory in the East. Not many wineries have been in existence long enough to have accumulated reds with more than a few years' age, and even fewer of these older wines are available for sale. It will take more experience to tell how long some of these premium Eastern reds will continue to improve or when they will reach their peak.

Another exciting area being explored today is the blending of two or more grape varieties. Some of the world's best known reds — those of Bordeaux come quickly to mind — are blends perfected through a long period of experimentation. Many people believe that in the East, too, skillful blending will produce the prominent red wines of the future.

Maréchal Foch

Foch has been called the "workhorse" of Eastern red varieties because of its widespread use for many types of wine. It can produce a deep-colored, heavy-bodied varietal; it is often used in blends; and a newer trend has been to make Foch in a more delicate, fruity, Beaujolais style, sometimes marketed as a nouveau.

Chancellor

Often used to produce big, Rhone-like wines, Chancellor has been described as spicy and buttery, with elements of cloves and cinnamon. It is also made in a lighter style, and many interesting Eastern reds blend Chancellor with another variety.

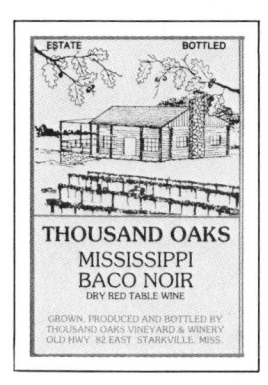

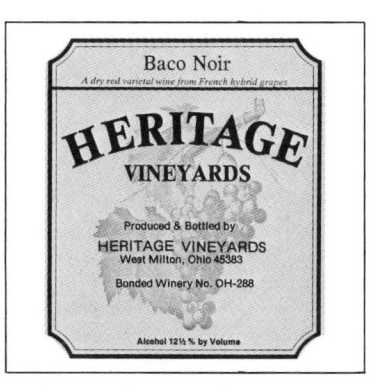

Baco Noir

Baco Noir has a pretty, berry-like quality that has been termed "plummy." It is one of the best aging wines in the East, making it valuable for blends. With age Baco takes on a toasty, burnt sugar characteristic.

De Chaunac

The heavy-bodied inky style of past De Chaunacs has been replaced by hearty and deep-colored wines with a spicy tobacco flavor. In Ontario, De Chaunac is being made in quantity as a white wine for blending.

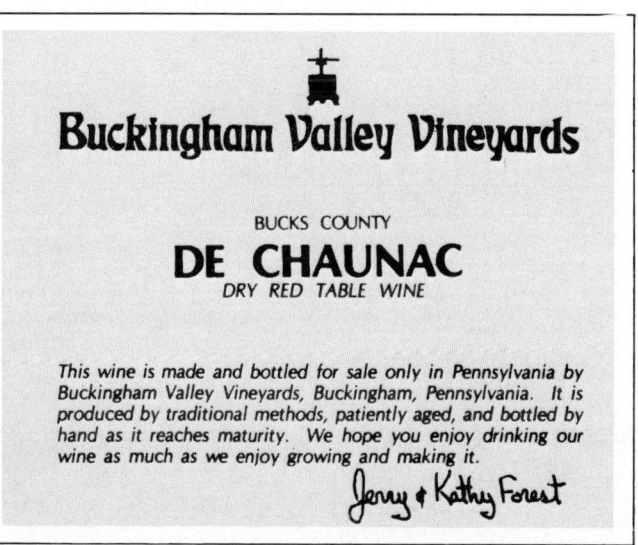

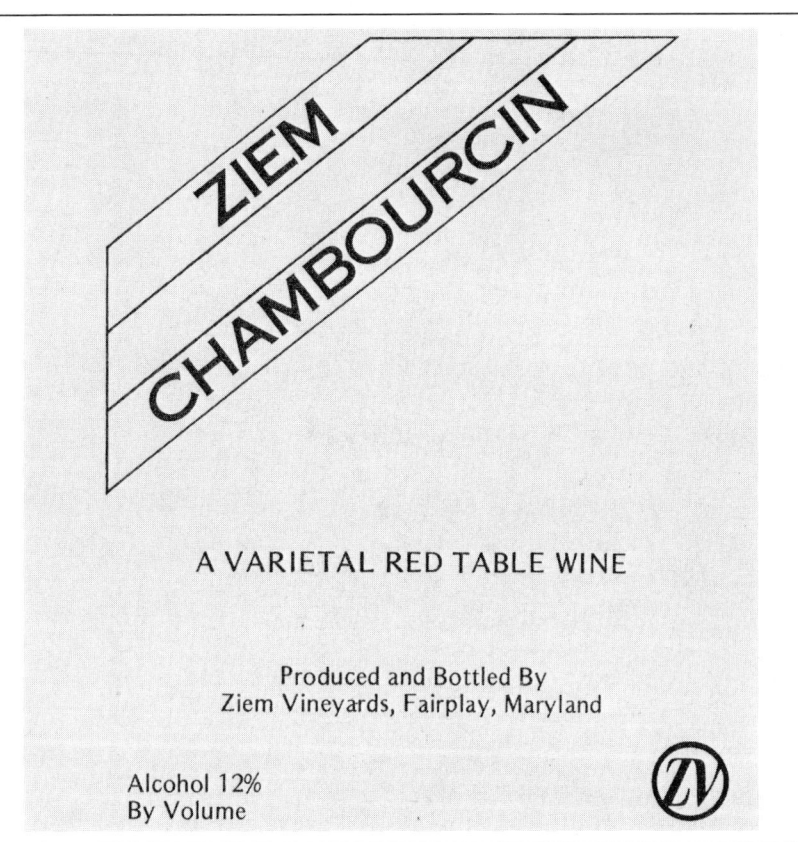

Chelois

Chelois is a medium-bodied wine that can often be identified by a prominent cedar-like nose. It has good aging potential, and adds style and finish to many red blends.

Chambourcin

Plantings of Chambourcin are on the increase, and wines made from this variety are fast gaining in popularity. The refined, subdued flavor and complex elements of Chambourcin, with hints of dill and green peppers, have led to a description of the wine as being "somewhere between Cabernet Sauvignon and Pinot Noir."

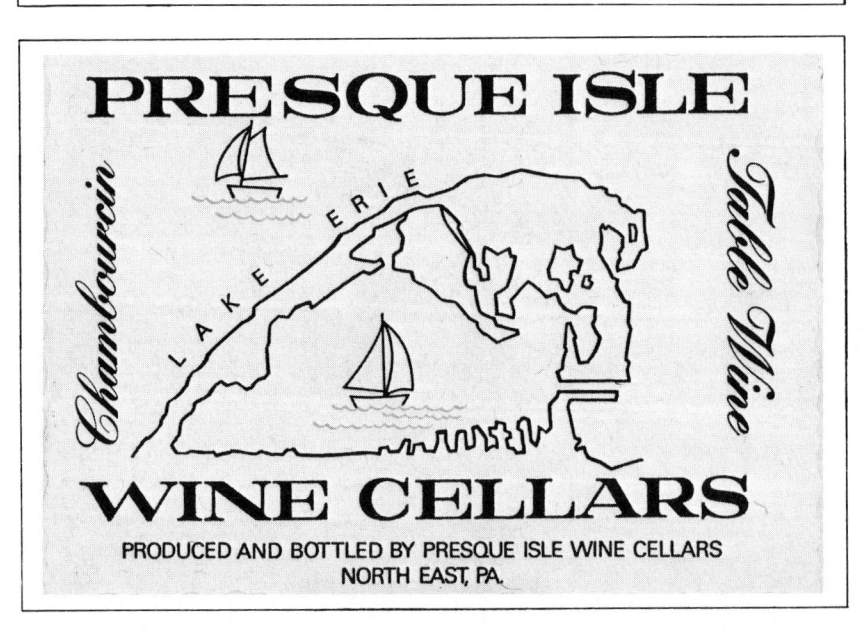

Cabernet Sauvignon

The name Cabernet Sauvignon signifies prestige wherever it is made. Eastern Cabernets are not as forward as their California counterparts, and their higher natural acidity lends a firm backbone to the wines. Not many Cabernets are presently made in the East, but the number is steadily increasing.

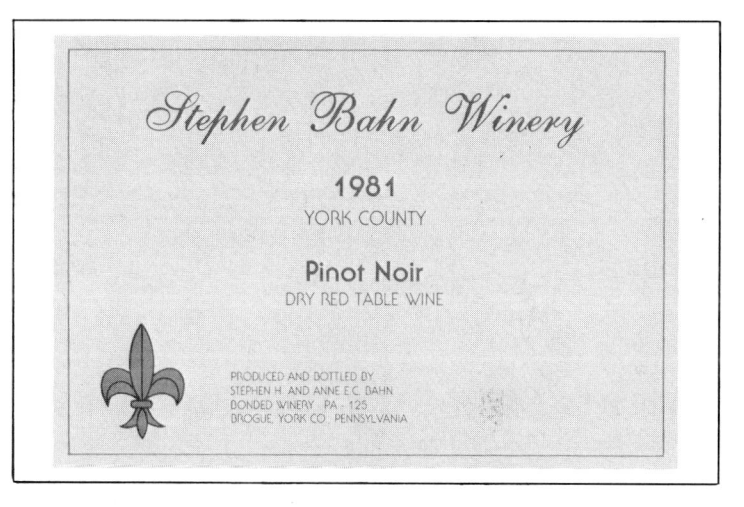

Pinot Noir

Eastern Pinot Noirs are light, clean and berry-like, more similar to Swiss and German reds than to the Pinot Noirs of Burgundy. While the wines show promise, Pinot Noir is a difficult variety to grow and the number of sites where it has been successfully grown in the East is, as of now, limited.

Other Reds

Among other reds made in the East are Léon Millot and Cascade, both resembling Foch in their full body and deep color. Seen less frequently are Villard Noir, another big bodied wine, and Landot, a lighter wine with delicate fruit. Concord, a major grape for the juice industry, has a grapey flavor and is used for sweeter wines.

Rosés

While many Eastern rosés are light versions of the prominent red varieties such as Chancellor, Foch or Chambourcin, there are a few varieties identified primarily with rosé wines. Two successful ones are Steuben and Rougeon. The many light pink Catawbas made in the East also fit into the rosé category.

CHARAL

CHANDELLE ROSÉ

11% alc./vol.   750 mL

Rosé wine - Vin rosé

A blend of premium wines, selected from our cellars, pleasantly dry, fresh and fruity.

Product of Canada — Produit du Canada

**Charal Winery & Vineyards Inc.
Blenheim, Ontario, Canada**

Byrd

1981
CHURCH HILL
AMERICAN
ROSÉ TABLE WINE

A medium sweet Wine

produced and bottled by
Byrd Vineyards, Myersville, Maryland

Alcohol 11% by Volume

Jucquan Vineyard

Steuben
Table Wine

Grown, produced, and bottled with care by
Thomas M. and Lucinda E. Hampton
R.D. 2, Holtwood, PA

SOUTH CAROLINA

Rosé de Chambourcin
1981

A delightful, fruity rosé wine, so very common in Europe. Made from the free run juice of the Chambourcin grape, fermented cold to insure the floral aroma of the grape.

Alcoholic Contents 12% By Volume

PRODUCED AND BOTTLED BY

Truluck ♣ Vineyards

BW-SC-8, ROUTE 3, LAKE CITY, SOUTH CAROLINA, U.S.A.

FISHER RIDGE VINEYARD

Choix du Cochon
(Limited Selection)

Table Wine
Produced and Bottled by Fisher Ridge Wine Company
Liberty, West Virginia 25124 BW-WV-2

Choix du Cochon. These wines are the personal project of Fisher Ridge winemaker and owner Dr. Wilson E. Ward. The grapes come exclusively from the Fisher Ridge Vineyard and are produced in extremely small quantities. The wines are for sale only in West Virginia.

Tri-Mountain

VINTAGE 1983

Virginia Table Wine

Seyval – Aligoté

Produced and Bottled by
TRI-MOUNTAIN WINERY and VINEYARDS INC.
Middletown, Virginia 22645 BW-VA-39

Seyval-Aligoté is a dry white blended wine vinified in the Burgundian style and aged in oak barrels. Seyval-Aligoté is produced from the Aligoté grape, a vinifera grape coming from the region of Burgundy in France, and from the Seyval grape, a French Hybrid showing great promise here in Virginia and Tri-Mountain Vineyards in the cradle of three mountains—the Blue Ridge to the East, the Massanutten to the South, and the Great North Mountain to the West—in the heart of the Shenandoah Valley.

Nittany Valley Winery

Coeur du Lion
"Heart of the Lion"
Soft Red Table Wine

Produced and Bottled by Nittany Valley Winery

| State College, Pennsylvania | BW-PA-120 | Frank R. Johns, Vintner |

Sakonnet

RHODE ISLAND TABLE WINE
CHILLABLE RED

A medium-dry, light red wine blended entirely from French hybrid grapes. Grown, produced and bottled by Sakonnet Vineyards, Little Compton, Rhode Island. Alcohol 12.5% by volume.

ESTATE BOTTLED

1978

Mountain Cove Vineyards

VIRGINIA

SKYLINE RED

1981

Table Wine Grown, Produced and Bottled
by La Abra Farm & Winery, Inc.
Lovingston, Va. 22949

Mountain Cove Vineyards are located in the foothills of the Blue Ridge Mountains of Virginia. Our climate and soil provide an environment in which fine grapes prosper. All of our vines are within sight of the winery, enabling us to pick and crush the grapes at optimum ripeness to make the best possible wine.

— Wingrower

This wine was made from freshly crushed grapes, pressed, and fermented in our own cellars. During aging the wine is clarified by settling and racking, and is filtered before bottling. SO₂, to prevent the growth of harmful organisms, is used during production. In some vintages, sugar and filter aids may be needed.

Hermannhof

FROM HISTORIC HERMANN — THE MISSOURI RHINELAND

The Village of Hermann

GENERATIONS OF VINICULTURE
GO INTO HERMANNHOF WINES

OAKEN CASKS IN STONE CELLARS
NURTURE OUR SUPERB WINES

ESTABLISHED 1852

THE IMMIGRANT'S LEGENDARY
SETTLER'S PRIDE

A SWEET WHITE WINE   SERVE CHILLED

MADE & BOTTLED BY HERMANNHOF WINERY, BW 106
330 E. FIRST ST., HERMANN, MO 65041. FOR INFORMATION ABOUT INGREDIENTS
IN THIS PRODUCT, WRITE HERMANNHOF WINERY.

Non-Varietal Wines, House Blends & Proprietary Labels

Most wineries in the East make both varietal wines, identified as such on the label, and other non-varietal wines. The majority of the non-varietal wines are blends of two or more grape varieties. While some of these blends are planned and purposely executed to achieve a desired result by combining the best elements of several varieties, others are the winery's "house" wine — a mixture of whatever grapes or wines are not used elsewhere.

Non-varietal blends may be designated in a number of ways. Some are labelled simply as "red table wine" or "white table wine." Others carry creative proprietary names designed for regional identification and/or market appeal. Generic terms such as Sauterne, Chablis or Burgundy are more frequently used by the larger wineries in the East than by the smaller ones.

Varietals with a Past

Some unusual grape varieties used to make wine in the past may still be found in the East today. Often their use is confined to one winery or area where tradition or market demand justifies their continuance. Both the taste of some of these wines and their names would stump most wine experts.

STEUK'S
SANDUSKY
BLACK PEARL
DRY RED WINE
ALCOHOL 12% BY VOLUME
ESTATE BOTTLED
PRODUCED AND BOTTLED BY
THE STEUK WINE CO. SANDUSKY, OHIO 44870
BONDED WINERY #257

1883 FOUNDER FRANK QUALIA
TEXAS
LENOIR
ALCOHOL 11% BY VOLUME
PRODUCED AND BOTTLED BY
VAL VERDE WINERY
DEL RIO, TEXAS
Made From Fresh Grapes Grown in Our Own Vineyards

HERITAGE
HERITAGE Wine Cellars
PENNSYLVANIA
ISABELLA
ALCOHOL 12% BY VOLUME
PRODUCED AND BOTTLED FROM
100% PENNSYLVANIA GRAPES BY
HERITAGE WINE CELLARS
NORTH EAST, PENNSYLVANIA

MOUNT PLEASANT
STARK'S STAR
RED MISSOURI LIGHT WINE
PRODUCED AND BOTTLED BY
MOUNT PLEASANT VINEYARDS, AUGUSTA, MISSOURI
1978

BRONTE

Sister Lakes

HARTFORD LIGHT PORT

Michigan Light Port

*Made and Bottled by
Bronte Champagne & Wines Company, Inc.
At the Bronte Vineyards, Hartford, Michigan
Alcohol 16% by Volume*

BARDENHEIER

ANNIVERSARY BRAND
CALIFORNIA
GOLDEN MUSCATEL WINE

Fortified Wines: Port & Sherries

Many of the native American varieties grown in abundance in North America are well suited for the production of fortified wines such as ports and sherries. In the past they were a mainstay of the Eastern wine industry, when no dry table wines were being made. Following national trends, fortified wines account for a smaller percentage of the total market today than they once did. Fortified wines in the East are made almost exclusively by the very large wineries.

ESTABLISHED 1921 — BONDED WINERY 23

St Julian

PREMIUM MICHIGAN

VanBuren Dry Sherry

Pictured is The Van Buren County Courthouse, Paw Paw, Michigan. Built in 1901, this stately structure was designated a National Historical Building by the National Archives in 1979.

THIS CLASSIC DRY SHERRY CAPTURES THE AGELESS CHARM AND ELEGANCE OF THAT ERA IN OUR COUNTY'S PAST.

ALCOHOL 16% BY VOLUME

PROUDLY PRODUCED AND BOTTLED BY ST. JULIAN WINE CO. INC.
PAW PAW, VAN BUREN COUNTY, MICHIGAN BW 23

Brotherhood

AMERICA'S OLDEST WINERY

NEW YORK STATE

RUBY PORT

An ambrosial delight
to sip with dessert and after dinner

ALCOHOL 18% BY VOLUME

Made and Bottled by
THE BROTHERHOOD CORPORATION
Washingtonville, New York

Sparkling Wines

Historically, champagnes have been among the most important of Eastern wines. Until recently most were made by the larger wineries, but with today's wine boom in the East, many small premium wineries have taken a serious interest in champagne making. Other kinds of sparkling wines are also widely marketed in the East. Among the best selling have been the low alcohol sparkling wines sold under a variety of bird and animal names such as Cold Duck, Baby Duck and Pussycat. A recent addition has been a white wine spritzer produced in Canada.

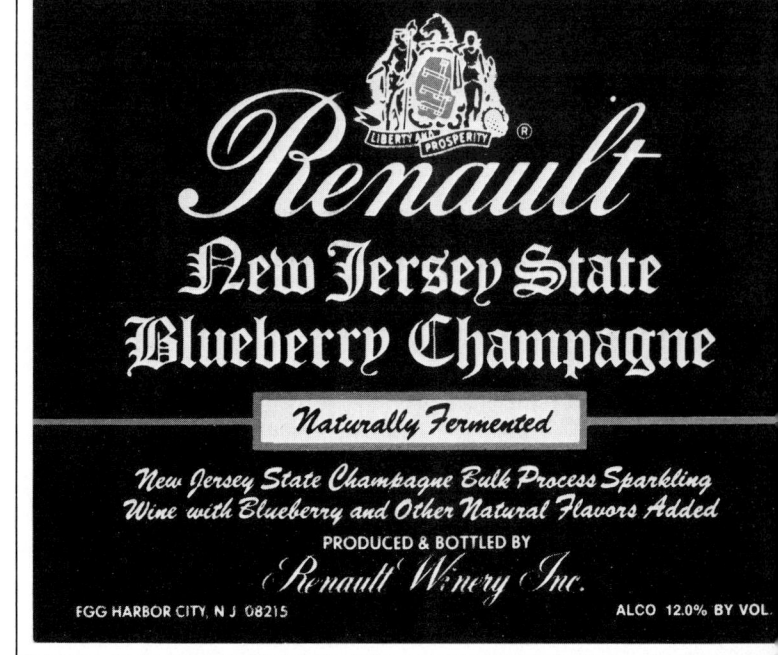

Chicama Vineyards

Sea Mist
Sparkling Wine

BRUT

Produced and Bottled by CHICAMA VINEYARDS
West Tisbury, Martha's Vineyard, Massachusetts

Alcohol 12% by volume   Fermented in this bottle

ANDRES

1.5 litre   7% alc./vol.

SPARKLING

BABY DUCK

Un Fin Mélange   A Fine Blend of
de Vins Rouges   Red and White
et Vins Blancs   Sparkling Wines

ANDRES WINES LTD., WINONA, CANADA

DUPLIN WINE CELLARS
VINTAGE WINE

Duplin Wine Cellars

Sparkling Scuppernong

(NORTH CAROLINA)

Naturally Fermented in this Bottle

CAUTION—THIS BOTTLE CONTAINS A LOT OF PRESSURE,
HANDLE CAREFULLY. PRODUCED AND BOTTLED BY
DUPLIN WINE CELLARS, ROSE HILL, NC. 28458
BW-NC-29 • ALCOHOL 12% BY VOLUME

Club Spritz

A unique refreshing blend of sparkling
white wine and pure spring water
Un mélange unique et rafraîchissant de vin blanc
mousseux et d'eau de source pure

750 ml

PRODUCT OF CANADA • T.G. BRIGHT & CO. LIMITED, NIAGARA FALLS, CANADA • PRODUIT DU CANADA

Fruit Wines

When wine is made from a fruit other than grapes, that wine must be designated by adding the name of the fruit to the word "wine." In the East, the popularity of fruit wines is on the increase. The most widely made is apple wine, produced by many small wineries as a complement to their product line. Substantial markets have also developed in recent years for strawberry, plum and nectarine wines. A few Eastern wineries market fruit wines exclusively.

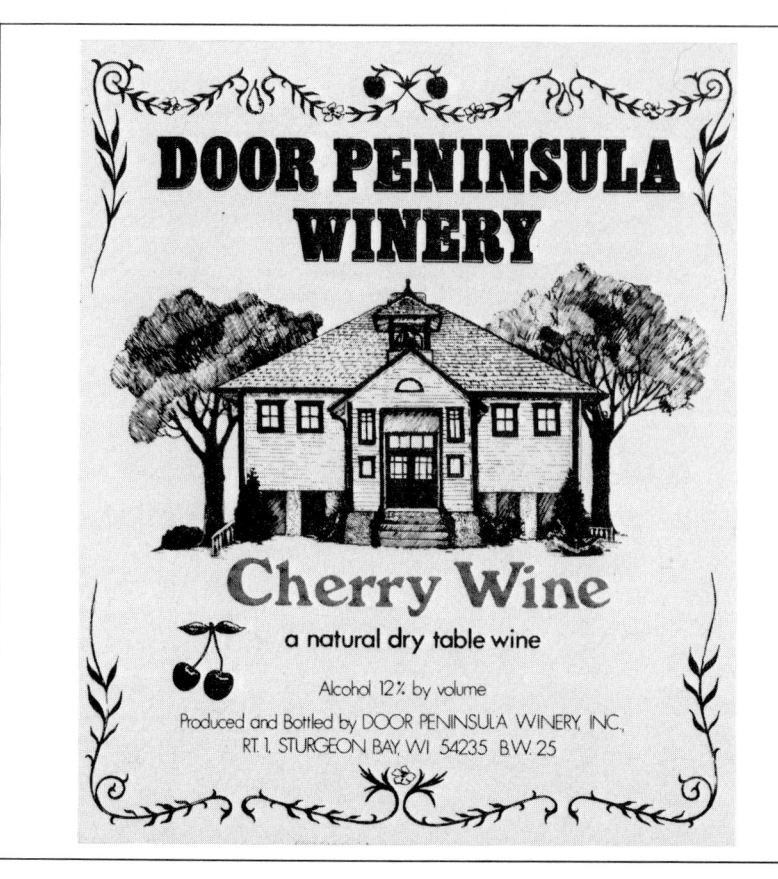

The Creative Touch

BENMARL

This label is to commemorate the marriage of Harriet Lee Stauffer and Eric Bruce Miller on January first, nineteen hundred and seventy-nine. (My mother thinks it took me so long it should be a national holiday.)

CUVÉE No. 27
1977
Estate Bottled
Hudson Region

This wine will ripen in two to five years.
Produced and bottled by the Benmarl Wine Co., Marlboro, N.Y.
750 ml, 12½% alcohol

Le Hamburgér Red

Cascade Mountain Vineyards
Table Wine

The name Le Hamburgér Red is our way of poking a little fun at American wines with fancy French names. But the wine itself, we hope you'll agree, is a laughing matter of another sort. It is a modestly priced wine suitable for just about any occasion and it's good. These days that's pretty funny.

William Wetmore

Produced and Bottled by Cascade Mountain Vineyard
Amenia, New York (914) 373-9021

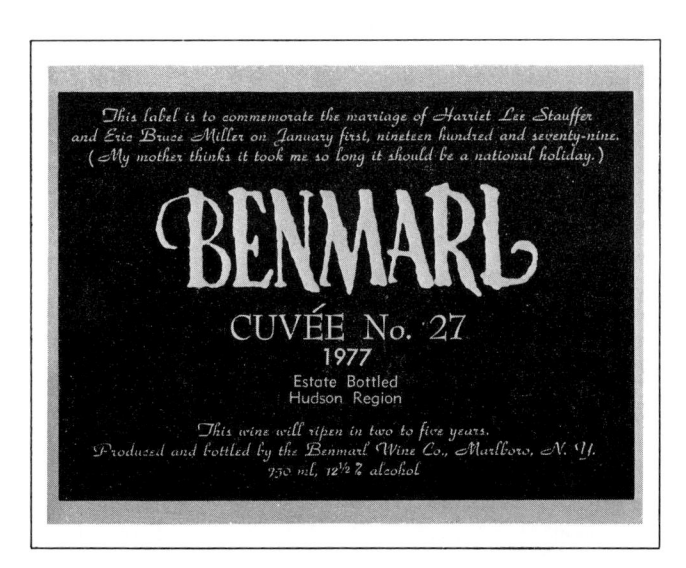

The individualism of a winery sometimes is apparent in the ways it presents itself to the public. Many wineries sell T-shirts, some of them as striking as the one marketed by Naked Mountain Vineyards of Markham, Virginia (see previous page). Signs used by wineries are often carefully designed to reflect the feelings the owners have about their wineries. It is in a winery's labels, perhaps, that the creative touch is most apparent. Labels have been expressly designed to commemorate a marriage; to mark such special events as an art exhibit; to identify a wine with a geographic area; or to associate a winery with a local tradition, as Lancaster County Winery chose to do when they adopted the red rose symbol of Lancaster, Pennsylvania. Humor plays its part and sometimes, as in the case of Naylor Wine Cellars, a lighthearted idea becomes popular with customers and simply takes off. The "war" depicted on Naylor's Grenadier labels was interrupted by a Christmas truce.

TEXAS GOLD

PREMIUM RED
red table wine

PRODUCED AND BOTTLED
IN TEXAS BY
La Buena Vida Vineyards
WSR BOX 18-3 ★ SPRINGTOWN ★ TEXAS ★ 76082

ALCOHOL 11% BY VOLUME

Lancaster County Winery

Colonial Red Wine

A mellow, rich grape wine with a distinctive aroma and flavor. Serve chilled or iced.

Alcohol 12% by Volume

Produced & Bottled by

Lancaster County Winery, Ltd.
Willow Street Pa 17584

RUBY GRENADIER

YORK COUNTY

SUGAR PLUM

Socially Sweet
Rosé Table Wine

GROWN, PRODUCED AND BOTTLED BY
NAYLOR WINE CELLARS, INC.
STEWARTSTOWN, PENNSYLVANIA

MOUNT HOPE

ART FESTIVAL RED WINE

Pennsylvania

% alcohol by volume. Produced and bottled by Mount [Ho]pe Estate and Winery, Cornwall, PA 17016. PA-BW-89.

GOLDEN GRENADIER

YORK COUNTY
APFELWEIN
Socially Sweet
Delicate Apple Wine
Alcohol 11% by volume
GROWN, PRODUCED AND BOTTLED BY
NAYLOR WINE CELLARS, INC.
STEWARTSTOWN, PENNSYLVANIA

RUBY GRENADIER

YORK COUNTY
FRAGOLA
Socially Sweet
Delicate Strawberry Wine
Alcohol 11% by volume
GROWN, PRODUCED AND BOTTLED BY
NAYLOR WINE CELLARS, INC.
STEWARTSTOWN, PENNSYLVANIA

RUBY GRENADIER

YORK COUNTY
FRAMBOISE
Socially Sweet
Delicate Raspberry Wine
Alcohol 11% by volume
GROWN, PRODUCED AND BOTTLED BY
NAYLOR WINE CELLARS, INC.
STEWARTSTOWN, PENNSYLVANIA

GOLDEN GRENADIER

YORK COUNTY
NIAGARA
Socially Sweet
White Table Wine
Alcohol 11% by volume
PRODUCED AND BOTTLED BY
NAYLOR WINE CELLARS, INC.
STEWARTSTOWN, PENNSYLVANIA

154

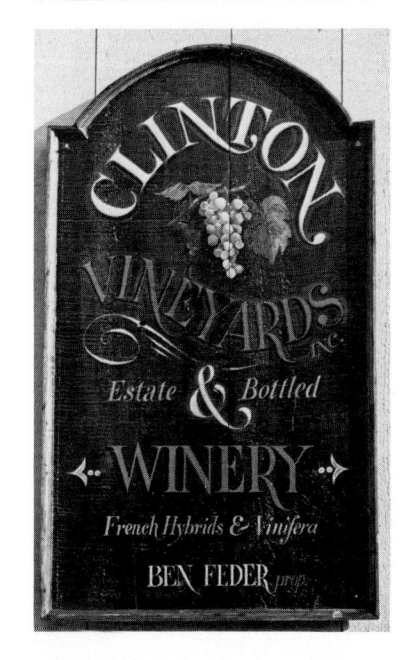

Appendix:
The Wineries
of the East

ALABAMA

Perdido Vineyards, Rt. 1, Box 20-A, Perdido, AL 36562 (205) 937-WINE

ARKANSAS

Cowie Wine Cellars, P.O. Box 284, Paris, AR 72855; (501) 963-3990

Heckmann's Winery, Rt. 1, Box 148, Harrisburg, AR 72432; (501) 578-5541.

Mount Bethel Winery, P.O. Box 137, U.S. Hwy. 64, Altus, AR 72821; (501) 468-2444

Neil's Winery, Rt. 1, Springdale, AR 72764; (501) 361-2954

Post Winery, Rt. 1, Box 1, Altus, AR 72821; (501) 468-2741

Henry J. Sax, Rt. 1, Altus, AR 72821; (501) 468-2332

Wiederkehr Wine Cellars, Rt. 1, Box 9, Altus, AR; (501) 468-2611

COLORADO

Colorado Mountain Vineyards, 3553 East Rd., Palisade, CO 81526

CONNECTICUT

Haight Vineyards, Chestnut Hill, Litchfield, CT 06759; (203) 567-4045

Hamlet Hill Vineyards, Pomfret, CT 06258; (203) 928-5550

Hopkins Vineyards, Hopkins Rd., New Preston, CT 06777; (203) 868-7954

St. Hilary's Vineyard, R.F.D. 1, North Grosvenordale, CT 06255; (203) 935-5377

Stonecrop Vineyards, R.D. 2, Box 151A, Stonington, CT 06378; (203) 535-2497

DELAWARE

Northminster Winery, 215 Stone Crop, Wilmington, DE 19810; (302) 774-1801

FLORIDA

Alaqua Vineyard, Rt. 1, Box 97-04, Freeport, FL 32439; (904) 678-7363

Florida Heritage Winery, Box 116, Anthony, FL 32617

Fruit Wines of Florida, 513 S. Florida Ave., Tampa, FL 33602; (813) 223-1222/226-3221

GEORGIA

Happy "B" Farm Winery, Rt. 4, Box 447, Forsyth, GA 31029; (912) 994-6549

Monarch Wine Co. of Georgia, 451 Sawtell Ave., SE, Atlanta, GA 30315; (404) 622-4496

ILLINOIS

Gem City Vineland Co., S. Parley St., Nauvoo, IL 62354; (217) 453-2218

Lynfred Winery, 15 S. Roselle Rd., Roselle, IL 60172; (312) 529-1000

Thompson Winery, P.O. Box 127, Monee, IL 60449; (312) 534-8050

INDIANA

Easley Enterprises, 205 N. College Ave., Indianapolis, IN 46202; (317) 636-4516

Golden Rain Tree Winery, R. R. 2, Wadesville, IN 47638; (812) 963-6441

Huber Orchard Winery, Rt. 1, Box 202, Borden, IN 47106; (812) 923-WINE

Oliver Wine Company, 8024 North Hwy. 37, Bloomington, IN 47401; (812) 876-5800

Possum Trot Vineyards, 8310 N. Possum Trot Rd., Unionville, IN 47468; (812) 988-2694

Swiss Valley Vineyards, 101 S. Ferry, Vevay, IN 47043; (513) 521-5096

IOWA

Ackerman Winery, South Amana, IA 52334; (319) 622-3379

Christina Wine Cellars, 123 A St., McGregor, IA 52157; (319) 873-3321

Colony Village Winery, I-80, Exit 55, Williamsburg, IA; (319) 622-3379

Colony Wines, Amana, IA 52203; (319) 668-2712

Der Weinkeller, Box 172A, Amana, IA 52203; (319) 622-3630

Ehrle Brothers Winery, Homestead, IA 52236; (319) 622-3241

Little Amana Winery, Box 172A, I-80, Amana, IA 52203: (319) 668-1011

Okoboji Winery, Hwy. 71, Okoboji, IA 51355; (712) 332-2674

Old Style Colony Winery, Middle Amana, IA 52037; (319) 622-3451

Old Wine Cellar Winery, Amana, IA 52203; (319) 622-3117

Private Stock Winery, 706-708 Allen, Boone, IA 50036; (515) 432-8348

Sandstone Winery, Box 7, Amana, IA 52203; (319) 622-3081

Village Winery, Amana, IA 52203; (319) 622-3448

KENTUCKY

Andrew Berg Cellars, 310 E. Broadway Ave., Bardstown, KY; (502) 897-1911

Colcord Winery, Third & Pleasant St., Paris, KY 40361; (606) 987-7440

Laine Vineyards & Winery, Rt. 5, Box 247, Fulton, KY 42041; (502) 472-3345

MARYLAND

Berrywine Plantations, Glisans Mill Rd., Box 247, Route 4, Mt. Airy, MD 21771; (301) 662-8687

Boordy Vineyards, 12820 Long Green Pike, Hydes, MD 21082; (301) 592-5015

Byrd Vineyards, Church Hill Rd., Myersville, MD 21773; (301) 293-1110

Montbray Wine Cellars, Ltd., 818 Silver Run Valley Rd., Westminster, MD 21157; (301) 346-7878

Provenza Vineyards, 805 Greenbridge Rd., Brookeville, MD 20729; (301) 277-2447

Ziem Vineyards, Rt. 1, Fairplay, MD 21733; (301) 223-8352

MASSACHUSETTS

Chicama Vineyards, Stoney Hill Rd., West Tisbury, MA 02575; (617) 693-0309

Commonwealth Winery, Cordage Park, Plymouth, MA 02360; (617) 746-4138

Nashoba Valley Winery, Damonmill Square, Concord, MA 01742; (617) 369-0885

MICHIGAN

Boskydel Vineyard, Rt. 1, Box 522, Lake Leelanau, MI 49653; (616) 256-7272

Bronte Champagne & Wines Co., Rt. 2, Hartford, MI 49057; (616) 621-3419

Chateau Grand Travers, Ltd., 12239 Center Rd., Traverse City, MI 49684; (616) 223-7355

Chi Company (Tabor Hill Vineyard), Rt. 2, Box 720, Buchanan, MI 49107; (616) 422-1161

Fenn Valley Vineyards, Rt. 4, 6130 122nd Ave., Fennville, MI 49408; (616) 561-2396

Fink Winery, 208 Main St., Dundee, MI 48131; (313) 529-3296

Frontenac Vineyards, P.O. Box 215, 3418 W. Michigan Ave., Paw Paw, MI 49079; (616) 657-5531

Good Harbor Vineyards, Rt. 1, Box 891, Lake Leelanau, MI 49653; (616) 256-7165

Lakeside Vineyard, 13581 Red Arrow Hwy., Harbert, MI 49115; (616) 469-0700

L. Mawby Vineyards/Winery, P.O. Box 237, 4519 Elm Valley Rd., Suttons Bay, MI 49682; (616) 271-3522

Leelanau Wine Cellars, Ltd., 726 N. Memorial Hwy., Traverse City, MI 49684; (616) 946-1653

Milan Wineries, 4109 Joe St. at 6000 Michigan Ave., Detroit, MI 48210; (313) 894-6464
St. Julian Wine Co., 716 S. Kalamazoo St., Paw Paw, MI 49079; (616) 657-5568
Vendramino Vineyards, Rt. 1, Box 257, Paw Paw, MI 49079; (616) 657-5890
Warner Vineyards, 706 S. Kalamazoo St., Paw Paw, MI 49079; (616) 657-3165

MINNESOTA

Alexis Bailly Vineyards, 18200 Kirby, Hastings, MN 55033; (612) 437-1413
Lake Sylvia Vineyard, Rt. 1, Box 149, South Haven, MN 55382; (612) 236-7743

MISSISSIPPI

Almarla Vineyards, Frost Bridge Rd., Matherville, MS 39360; (601) 687-5548
Old South Winery, 507 Concord St., Natchez, MS 39120; (601) 445-9924
Thousand Oaks Vineyard & Winery, Rt. 4, Box 293, Starkville, MS 39759; (601) 323-6657
The Winery Rushing, Merigold, MS 38759; (601) 748-2731

MISSOURI

Ashby Vineyards (Rosati Winery), Rt. 1, Box 55, St. James, MO 65559; (314) 265-8629
Bardenheier's Wine Cellars, 1019 Skinker Pkwy., St. Louis, MO 63112; (314) 862-1400
Bias Vineyards & Winery, Rt. 1, Berger, MO 63014; (314) 834-5475
Bowman Wine Cellars, 500 Welt St., Weston, MO 64098; (816) 386-5588
Bristleridge Winery, Rt. 1, Knob Noster, MO 65336; (816) 747-5713
Carver Wine Cellars, Box 1316, Rolla, MO 65401; (314) 364-4335
Ferrigno Vineyards & Winery, Hwy. B, Rt. 1, Box 227, St. James, MO 65559; (314) 265-7742 (license pending)
Green Valley Vineyards, Hwy. D, Portland, MO 65067; (314) 676-5771
Heinrichshaus, Rt. 2, Box 139, St. James, MO 65559; (314) 265-5000
Hermannhof Winery, 330 E. First St., Hermann, MO 65041; (314) 486-5959
Kruger Winery and Vineyard, Rt. 1, Nelson, MO 65347; (816) 837-3217
Midi Vineyards, Rt. 1, Lone Jack, MO 64070; (816) 566-2119
Montelle Vineyards, Rt. 1, Box 94, Augusta, MO 63332; (314) 228-4464
Mount Pleasant Vineyards, 101 Webster St., Augusta, MO 63332; (314) 228-4419
Ozark Vineyard Winery, Chestnut Ridge, MO 65630; (417) 587-3555
Peaceful Bend Vineyard, Rt. 2, Box 131, Steelville, MO 65565; (314) 775-2578
Reis Winery, Rt. 4, Box 133, Licking, MO 65542; (314) 674-3763
St. James Winery, Rt. 2, Box 98A, St. James, MO 65559; (314) 265-7912
Stone Hill Wine Co., Rt. 1, Box 26, Hermann, MO 65041; (314) 486-2221
The Winery of the Abbey, Rt. 3, Box 199, Cuba, MO 65453; (314) 885-2168
Winery of the Little Hill, 208 Pittman Hill Rd., St. Charles, MO 63301; (314) 723-7313

NEW HAMPSHIRE

White Mountain Vineyards, RFD 2, Laconia, NH 03246; (603) 524-0174

NEW JERSEY

Antuzzi's Winery, Bridgeboro-Moorestown Rd., Delran, NJ 08075; (609) 764-1075
Balic Winery, Rt. 40, Mays Landing, NJ 08330; (609) 625-2166
DelVista Vineyards, Frenchtown Everittstown Rd., Frenchtown, NJ 08825; (201) 996-2849
Gross' Highland Winery, 212 Jim Leeds Rd., Absecon, NJ 08201; (609) 652-1187
Jacob Lee Winery, Rt. 130, Bordentown, NJ 08505; (609) 298-4860
Renault Winery, Bremen Ave., Egg Harbor City, NJ 08215; (609) 965-2111
Tewksbury Wine Cellars, Burrell Rd., Lebanon, NJ 08833; (201) 832-2400
Tomasello Winery, 225 N. White Horse Pike, Hammonton, NJ 08037; (609) 561-0567

NEW MEXICO

Corrales Bonded Winery, Box 302B, Corrales, NM 87048; (505) 898-2904
La Vina, Box 121, Chamberino, NM 88027; (505) 882-2092
Rico's Winery, 6406 N. 4th St., N.W., Albuquerque, NM 87107; (505) 344-2075
Vina Madre, Dexter, NM 88201; (505) 734-5590

NEW YORK

Americana Vineyards, 4367 E. Covert Rd., Interlaken, NY 14847; (607) 387-6801
The Barry Wine Co., 7107 Vineyard Rd., Conesus-on-Hemlock Lake, NY 14435; (716) 346-2321
Benmarl Wine Company, Highland Ave., Marlboro, NY 12542; (914) 236-7271
Bluff Point Winery, RD 5, Vine Rd., Penn Yan, NY 14527; (315) 536-2682
Brimstone Hill Vineyard, Brimstone Hill Rd., Pine Bush, NY 12566; (914) 744-2231
Brotherhood Corporation, 35 North St., Washingtonville, NY 10992; (914) 496-3661
Bully Hill Vineyards, Greyton H. Taylor Memorial Dr., Hammondsport, NY 14840; (607) 868-3610
Cagnasso Winery, Rt. 9W, Marlboro, NY 12542; (914) 236-4630
Canandaigua Wine Company, 116 Buffalo St., Canandaigua, NY 14424; (716) 394-3630
Casa Larga Vineyards, 27 Emerald Hill Circle, Fairport, NY 14450; (716) 223-3034
Cascade Mountain Vineyards, Flint Hill Rd., Amenia, NY 12501; (914) 373-9021
Chadwick Bay Wine Company, 10001 Route 60, Fredonia, NY 14063; (716) 672-5000
Chateau Esperanza, Rt. 54A, Bluff Point, NY 14417; (315) 536-7481
Clinton Vineyards, Schultzville Rd., Clinton Corners, NY 12514; (914) 266-5372
Cottage Vineyards, Box 608, Marlboro-on-the-Hudson, NY 12542; (914) 236-4870
Crown Royal Wine Cellars, 657 Montgomery St., Brooklyn, NY 11225; (212) 467-6218
De May Wine Cellars, Rt. 88, Hammondsport, NY 14840; (607) 569-2040
Eaton Vineyards, P.O. Box 284, Pine Plains, NY 12567; (518) 398-7791
El Paso Winery, R.D. 1, Box 170, Ulster Park, NY 12487; (914) 331-8642
Finger Lakes Wine Cellars, Italy Hill Rd., Branchport, NY 14418; (315) 595-2812
Four Chimneys Farm Winery, Hall Rd., Himrod, NY 14842; (607) 243-7502
Galante's Farm Winery, 9813 Erie Rd., Angola, NY 14006; (716) 549-0634
Giasi Winery, Box 72B, Rt. 414, Burdett, NY 14818; (607) 546-4601
Glenora Wine Cellars, Hwy. 14, Glenora-on-Seneca, Dundee, NY 14837; (607) 243-7600
Gold Seal Vineyards, Rt. 54A, Hammondsport, NY 14840; (607) 868-3232

Hammondsport Wine Company, 89 Lake St., Hammondsport, NY 14840; (607) 569-2255

Heron Hill Vineyards, Middle Rd., Hammondsport, NY 14840; (607) 868-4241

Hi Tor Vineyards, Hi Tor Rd., New City, NY 10956; (914) 634-7960 (license pending)

Hudson Valley Wine Company, Blue Point Rd., Highland, NY 12528; (914) 691-7296

Frederick S. Johnson Vineyards, W. Main Rd., Box 52, Westfield, NY 14787; (716) 326-2191

Long Island Vineyards, Alvah's Lane, Box 927, Cutchogue, LI, NY 11935; (516) 734-5158

Lucas Winery, R.D. 2, County Rd. 150, Interlaken, NY 14847; (607) 532-4825

McGregor Vineyards, 5503 Dutch St., Dundee, NY 14837; (607) 292-3999

Merritt Estate Winery, 2264 King Rd., Forestville, NY 14062; (716) 965-4800

Mogen David Wine Corp., 85 Bourne St., P.O. Box 1, Westfield, NY 14787; (716) 326-3151

Monarch Wine Company, 4500 2nd Ave., Brooklyn, NY 11232; (212) 965-8800

Niagara Wine Cellars, 4100 Ridge Rd., Cambria, NY 14094; (716) 433-0856

Northeast Vineyard, Silver Mountain Rd., Millerton, NY 12546; (518) 789-3645

Northlake Vineyards, R.D. 1, Box 271, Romulus, NY 14541; (607) 273-6804

North Salem Vineyards, Hardscrabble & Delancey Rds., North Salem, NY 10560; (914) 669-5518

Penn Yan Wine Cellars, 150 Water St., Penn Yan, NY 14527; (315) 536-2361

Plane's Cayuga Vineyard, R.D. 2, Rt. 89, Ovid, NY 14521; (607) 869-5158

Pleasant Valley Wine Company, Hammondsport, NY 14840; (607) 569-2121

Poplar Ridge Vineyards, R. D. 1, Rt. 414, Valois, NY 14888; (607) 582-6421

Robin Fils & Cie., Ltd., School St. & Hewitt Pl., Batavia, NY 14020; (716) 344-1111

Rolling Vineyards Farm Winery, P.O. Box 37, 5055 Rt. 414, Hector, NY 14841; (607) 546-9302

Rotolo & Romeo Wines, 234 Rochester St., Avon, NY 14414; (716) 226-2760

Royal Wine Corp., Dock Rd., Milton, NY 12547; (914) 795-2240

Schapiro's Wine Company, 126 Rivington St., New York, NY 10002; (212) 674-4404

Schloss Doepken Winery, E. Main Rd., RD 2, Ripley, NY 14775; (716) 326-3636

The Taylor Wine Company, Hammondsport, NY 14840; (607) 569-2111

Valley Vineyards, Oregon Trail Rd., Walker Valley, NY 12588; (914) 744-3912/5287

Villa D'Ingianni Winery, 1183 E. Keuka Lake Rd., Rt. 54, Dundee, NY 14837; (607) 292-3814

Vinifera Wine Cellars, R. D. 2, Hammondsport, NY 14840; (607) 868-4884

Wagner Vineyards, Rt. 414, Lodi, NY 14860; (607) 582-6450

Wickham Vineyards, 1 Wine Pl., Box 62, Hector, NY 14841; (607) 546-8415

Hermann J. Wiemer Vineyard, Box 4, Dundee, NY 14837; (607) 243-7971

Widmer's Wine Cellars, West Ave. & Tobey St., Naples, NY 14512; (716) 374-6311

Windmill Farms, 193 County Line Rd., Ontario, NY 14519

Windsor Vineyards (Great River Winery, Marlboro Champagne Cellars), 104 Western Ave., Marlboro, NY 12542; (914) 236-4440

Woodbury Vineyards, Rt. 1, South Roberts Rd., Dunkirk, NY 14048; (716) 679-1708

NORTH CAROLINA

Biltmore Estate, P.O. Box 5375, Asheville, NC 28803; (704) 274-1776

Duplin Wine Cellars, P.O. Box 268, Rose Hill, NC 28458; (919) 289-3888

Germanton Vineyard & Winery, RFD 1, Box 1-6, Germanton, NC 27019; (919) 969-5745

LaRocca Wine Company, 408 Buie Ct., Fayetteville, NC 28304; (919) 484-8865

OHIO

Breitenbach Wine Cellars, R.R. 1, Dover, OH 44622; (216) 343-3603

Leslie J. Bretz, P.O. Box 17, Middle Bass, OH 43446; (419) 285-2323

Brushcreek Vineyards, 12351 Newkirk Ln., Peebles, OH 45660; (513) 588-2618

Buccia Vineyards, 518 Gore Rd., Conneaut, OH 44030

Cedar Hill Wine Co., 2195 Lee Rd., Cleveland Heights, OH 44118; (216) 321-9511

Chalet Debonne Vineyards, 7743 Doty Rd., Madison, OH 44057; (216) 466-3485

John Christ Winery, 32421 Walker Rd., Avon Lake, OH 44012; (216) 933-3046

Colonial Vineyards, 6222 N. State Rt. 48, Lebanon, OH 45036; (513) 932-3842

Daughters Wine Cellar, 5573 N. Ridge Rd., Madison, OH 44057; (216) 428-5138

Dover Vineyards, 24945 Detroit Rd., Westlake, OH 44145; (216) 871-0700

E & K Wine Co., 220 E. Water St., Sandusky, OH 44870; (419) 627-9622

Ferrante Wine Farm, 5585 Route 307 West, Harpersfield, Geneva, OH 44041

Grand River Wine Co., 5750 Madison Rd., Madison, OH 44057

Granville Vineyards, P.O. Box 497, Granville, OH 43023; (614) 587-0312

Hafle Vineyards, 2369 Upper Valley Pike, Springfield, OH 45502; (513) 399-2334

Heineman Winery, Put-in-Bay, OH 43456; (419) 285-2811

Heritage Vineyards, 6020 S. Wheelock Rd., W. Milton, OH 45383; (513) 698-5369

Louis Jindra Winery, 2701 Camba Rd. C.R. 15, Jackson, OH 45640; (614) 286-6578

Johlin Winery, 3935 Corduroy Rd., Oregon, OH 43616; (419) 693-6288

Klingshirn Winery, 33050 Weber Rd., Avon Lake, OH 44012; (216) 933-6666

Carl M. Limpert, 28083 Detroit Rd., Westlake, OH 44145; (216) 871-0035

Mantey Vineyards, 917 Bardshar Rd., Sandusky, OH 44870; (419) 625-5474

Markko Vineyard, R. D. 2, S. Ridge Rd., Conneaut, OH 44030; (216) 593-3197

Marlo Winery, 3660 State Rt. 47, Fort Loramie, OH 45845; (513) 295-3232

McIntosh's Ohio Valley Wines, 2033 Bethel New Hope Rd., Bethel, OH 45106; (513) 379-1159

Meier's Wine Cellars, 6955 Plainfield Pike, Silverton, Cincinnati, OH 45236; (513) 891-2900

Mon Ami Champagne Company, 3845 E. Wine Cellars Rd., Catawba Island, Port Clinton, OH 43452; (419) 797-4482

Moyer Vineyards, U.S. Hwy. 52, Manchester, OH 45144; (513) 549-2957

Pompei Winery, 3995 E. 86th St., Cleveland, OH 44105; (216) 883-9370

Steuk Wine Company, 1001 Fremont Ave., Sandusky, OH 44870; (419) 625-0803

Still Water Wineries, 2311 State Rt. 55 West, Troy, OH 45373; (513) 339-8346

Stone Quarry Vineyards Winery, Box 142, Waterford, OH 45786; (614) 984-4423

Tarula Farms, 1786 Creek Rd., Clarksville, OH 45113; (513) 289-2181

Valley Vineyards Farm, 2041 E. U.S. 22-3, Morrow, OH 45152; (513) 899-2485

Vinterra Farms, 6505 Stoker Rd., Houston, OH 45333; (513) 492-2071

Wickliffe Winery, 29555 (Rear) Euclid Ave., Wickliffe, OH 44092; (216) 943-1030

Willoughby Winery, 30829 Euclid Ave., Willowick, OH 44092; (216) 943-5405

Wyandotte Wine Cellar, 4640 Wyandotte Dr., Gahanna, OH 43230; (614) 476-3624

OKLAHOMA

Arrowhead Vineyards, Rt. 1, Caney, OK 74533; (405) 889-6312

Pete Schwarz Winery, Box 545, Okarche, OK 73762; (405) 263-7664

PENNSYLVANIA

Adams County Winery, Peach Tree Rd., R.D. 1, Ortanna, PA 17353; (717) 334-4631

Allegro Vineyards, R. D. 2, Box 64, Brogue, PA 17309; (717) 927-9148

Brandywine Vineyards, Rt. 896, Kemblesville, PA 19347; (215) 255-4171

Buckingham Valley Vineyards, Box 371, Rt. 413, Buckingham, PA 18912; (215) 794-7188

Bucks Country Vineyards, R.D. 1, New Hope, PA 18938; (215) 794-7449

Buffalo Valley Winery, Buffalo Rd., Lewisburg, PA 17837; (717) 524-4850

Calvaresi Winery, 832 Thorn St., Reading, PA 19601; (215) 373-7821

Chadds Ford Winery, Rt. 1, P.O. Box 229, Chadds Ford, PA 19317; (215) 388-6221

Conestoga Vineyards, 415 S. Queen St., Lancaster, PA 17603; (717) 393-0141

Country Creek Vineyard & Winery, 133 Cressman Rd., Telford, PA 18969; (215) 723-6516

Doerflinger Wine Cellars, 3248 Old Berwick Rd., Bloomsburg, PA 17815; (717) 784-2112

Dutch Country Wine Cellar, Rt. 143 North, Lenhartsville, PA 19534; (215) 756-6061

Heritage Wine Cellars, 12162 Buffalo Rd., North East, PA 16428; (814) 725-8015

Kolln Vineyards & Winery, Box 439, R.D. 1, Bellefonte, PA 16823; (814) 355-4666

Lancaster County Winery, Box 329, Willow Street, PA 17584; (717) 464-3555

Lapic Winery, 682 Tulip Dr., New Brighton, PA 15066; (412) 846-2031

Lembo's Vineyards, 34 Valley St., Lewistown, PA 17044; (717) 248-4078

Mazza Vineyards, 11815 E. Lake Rd., North East, PA 16428; (814) 725-8695

Mt. Hope Estate and Winery, P.O. Box 685, Cornwall, PA 17016; (717) 665-7021

Naylor Wine Cellars, Stewartstown, PA; (717) 993-2431

Neri's Wine Cellar, 373 Bridgetown Pike, Langhorne, PA 19047; (215) 355-9952

Nissley Vineyards, Rt. 1, Bainbridge, PA 17502; (717) 426-3514

Nittany Valley Winery, 724 S. Atherton St., State College, PA 16801; (814) 238-7562

Penn-Shore Vineyards, 10225 E. Lake Rd., North East, PA 16428; (814) 725-8688

Presque Isle Wine Cellars, 9440 Buffalo Rd., North East, PA 16428; (814) 725-1314

Quarry Hill Winery, R.D. 2, Box 168, Shippensburg, PA 17257; (717) 776-3411

Stephen Bahn Winery, Goram Rd., Brogue, PA 17309; (717) 927-9051

Tucquan Vineyard, R.D. 2, Box 20, Holtwood, PA 17532; (717) 284-2221

York Springs Winery, R.D. 1, Box 194, York Springs, PA 17372; (717) 528-8490

RHODE ISLAND

Diamond Hill Vineyard, 3145 Diamond Hill Rd., Cumberland, RI 02864; (401) 333-5642

Prudence Island Vineyards, Prudence Island, RI 02872; (401) 683-2452

Sakonnet Vineyards, W. Main Rd., Little Compton, RI 02837; (401) 635-4356

SOUTH CAROLINA

Truluck Vineyards, P.O. Drawer 1265, Rt. 3, Lake City, SC 29560; (803) 389-3400

TENNESSEE

Highland Manor Winery, Hwy. 127 South, Jamestown, TN 38556; (615) 879-9519

Smokey Mountain Winery, Brookside Village, Hwy. 73E, Gatlinburg, TN 37738; (615) 436-7551

Tiegs Vineyards, Jackson Bend Rd., Lenoir City, TN 37771; (615) 986-9949

TEXAS

Fall Creek Vineyards, Tow, TX 78672; (512) 476-3783

Glasscock Vineyards, P.O. Box 530, Fort Davis, TX 79734; (915) 426-3553

Guadalupe Valley Winery, 1720 Hunter Rd., New Braunfels, TX 78130; (512) 629-2351

La Buena Vida Vineyards, Springtown, TX 76082; (817) 523-4366

Llano Estacado (Staked Plains) Winery, Farm Rd. 1585, Lubbock, TX 79413; (806) 745-2258

Oberhellmann Vineyards, Llano Rt., Box 22, Fredericksburg, TX 78624; (512) 685-3297 (license pending)

Sanchez Creek Vineyard, DSR Box 30-4, Weatherford, TX 76086; (817) 594-6884

Val Verde Winery, 139 Hudson Dr., Del Rio, TX 78840; (512) 775-9714

VIRGINIA

Bacchanal Vineyards, Box 860, Rt. 2, Afton, VA 22920; (804) 272-6937

Barboursville Winery, P.O. Box F, Barboursville, VA 22923; (703) 832-3823

Blenheim Vineyards, Rt. 6, Box 75, Charlottesville, VA 22901; (804) 295-7666 (license pending)

Chermont Winery, Rt. 1, Box 59, Esmont, VA 22937; (804) 286-2639

Domaine de Gignoux, Box 48, Ivy, VA 22945; (804) 296-4101

Farfelu Vineyard, Flint Hill, VA 22627; (703) 364-2930

Ingleside Plantation Winery, Oak Grove, VA 22443; (804) 224-7111

La Abra Farm & Winery, Rt. 1, Box 139, Lovingston, VA 22949; (804) 263-5392

Meredyth Vineyard, Box 347, Middleburg, VA 22117; (703) 687-6277/6612

MJC Vineyard, Rt. 1, Box 293, Blacksburg, VA 24060; (703) 552-9083

Montdomaine Cellars, Rt. 6, Box 168A, Charlottesville, VA 22901; (804) 977-6120

Naked Mountain Vineyard, P.O. Box 131, Rt. 688, Markham, VA 22643; (703) 364-1609

Oasis Vineyards, Rt. 1, Hume, VA 22639; (703) 635-7627, 549-9181

Piedmont Vineyards & Winery, P.O. Box 286, Middleburg, VA 22117; (703) 687-5134

Rapidan River Vineyards, Rt. 4, Box 199, Culpeper, VA 22701; (703) 399-1855

Rose Bower Vineyard & Winery, P.O. Box 126, Hampden Sidney, VA 23943; (804) 223-8209

Shenandoah Vineyards, Rt. 2, Box 208B, Edinburg, VA 22824; (703) 984-8699

Tri-Mountain Winery, Box 254, Middletown, VA 22645; (703) 869-3030

The Vineyard, Rt. 5, Box 486Y, Winchester, VA 22601

Woolwine Winery, Box 100, Woolwine, VA 24185; (703) 745-3318

WEST VIRGINIA

Fisher Ridge Wine Company, Fisher Ridge Rd., Liberty, WV 25124; (304) 342-8701

Robert F. Pliska & Company Winery, Piterra, Purgitsville, WV 26852; (304) 289-3493

West-Whitehill Winery, Rt. 1, Box 247A, Keyser, WV 26726; (304) 788-3066

WISCONSIN

Christina Wine Cellars, 109 Vine St., La Crosse, WI 54601; (608) 785-2210

Door Peninsula Wine Co., Rt. 1, Sturgeon Bay, WI 54235; (414) 743-7431

Fruit of the Woods Wine Cellar, 1113 Wall St., Box 213, Eagle River, WI 54521; (715) 479-4800

Old Style Colony Winery, 608A Verona Ave., Verona, WI 53593

Renick Winery, 5600 Gordon Rd., Sturgeon Bay, WI 54235; (414) 743-7329

Stone Mill Winery, N. 70 W. 6340 Bridge Rd., Cedarburg, WI 53012; (414) 377-8020

Von Stiehl Wine, P.O. Box 45, 115 Navarino St., Algoma, WI 54201; (414) 487-5208

Wisconsin Winery, 529 Main St., Lake Geneva, WI 53147; (414) 248-3245

The Wollersheim Winery, Hwy. 188, Prairie Du Sac, WI 53578; (608) 643-6515

CANADA

ONTARIO

Andres Wines, P.O. Box 550, Winona, Ontario L0R 2L0; (416) 643-4131

Barnes Wines, P.O. Box 248, Martindale Rd., St. Catharines, Ontario L2R 6S4; (416) 682-6632

T. G. Bright & Co., P.O. Box 510, 4887 Dorchester Rd., Niagara Falls, Ontario; (416) 358-7141

Charal Winery & Vineyard, R.R. 1, Blenheim, Ontario N0P 1A0; (519) 676-3012

Chateau des Charmes Wines, R.R. 4, Niagara-on-the-Lake, Ontario L0S 1J0; (416) 262-5202

Chateau-Gai Wines, P.O. Box 360, Niagara Falls, Ontario L2E 6T8; (416) 354-1631

Colio Wines of Canada, Colio Dr., P.O. Box 372, Harrow, Ontario N0R 1G0; (519) 738-2241

Inniskillin Wines, Niagara Parkway, Niagara-on-the-Lake, Ontario; (416) 468-2187/2188

Jordan & Ste. Michelle Cellars, 120 Ridley Rd., St. Catharines, Ontario L2R 7E3; (416) 688-2140

London Winery, 560 Wharncliffe Rd. South, London, Ontario N6J 2N5; (519) 686-8431

Newark Wines, R.R. 2, Hwy. 55, Niagara-on-the-Lake, Ontario L0S 1J0; (416) 468-7123

Podamer Champagne Co., P.O. Box 968, Beamsville, Ontario L0R 1B0; (416) 563-8955/5313

Most of the wineries in this list offer tastings and most have tours. Some wineries may be closed on certain days of the week and some may have restricted hours during the winter; a call in advance is usually a good idea.

Below: Lapic Winery, New Brighton, Pennsylvania.